TALES OF BENGAL

First published 1910
This edition published by Lector House in 2023

ISBN: 978-93-5800-778-7

Lector House LLP
Registered Office: H. No. 96, Block C, Tomar Colony,
Burari, Delhi – 110084, India
info@lectorhouse.com
www.lectorhouse.com

TALES OF BENGAL

S. B. BANERJEA,
FRANCIS HENRY SKRINE

2023

LECTOR HOUSE LLP

TALES OF BENGAL

BY

S. B. BANERJEA

EDITED BY

FRANCIS HENRY SKRINE

INDIAN CIVIL SERVICE (RETIRED)

CONTENTS

INTRODUCTION.

That "east is east, and west is west, and never the twain shall meet," is an axiom with most Englishmen to whom the oriental character seems an insoluble enigma. This form of agnosticism is unworthy of a nation which is responsible for the happiness of 300,000,000 Asiatics. It is not justified by history, which teaches us that civilisation is the result of the mutual action of Europe and Asia; and that the advanced races of India are our own kinsfolk.

The scene of Mr. Banerjea's tales has been won from the sea by alluvial action. Its soil, enriched by yearly deposits of silt, yields abundantly without the aid of manure. A hothouse climate and regular rainfall made Bengal the predestined breeding-ground of mankind; the seat of an ancient and complex civilisation. But subsistence is too easily secured in those fertile plains. Malaria, due to the absence of subsoil drainage, is ubiquitous, and the standard of vitality extremely low. Bengal has always been at the mercy of invaders. The earliest inroad was prompted by economic necessity. About 2000 B.C. a congeries of races which are now styled "Aryan" were driven by the shrinkage of water from their pasture-grounds in Central Asia. They penetrated Europe in successive hordes, who were ancestors of our Celts, Hellenes, Slavs, Teutons and Scandinavians. Sanskrit was the Aryans' mother-tongue, and it forms the basis of nearly every European language. A later swarm turned the western flank of the Himalayas, and descended on Upper India. Their rigid discipline, resulting from vigorous group-selection, gave the invaders an easy victory over the negroid hunters and fishermen who peopled India. All races of Aryan descent exhibit the same characteristics. They split into endogamous castes, each of which pursues its own interests at the expense of other castes. From the dawn of history we find kings, nobles and priests riding roughshod over a mass of herdsmen, cultivators and artisans. These ruling castes are imbued with pride of colour. The Aryans' fair complexions differentiated them from the coal-black aborigines; *varna* in Sanskrit means "caste" and "colour". Their aesthetic instinct finds expression in a passionate love of poetry, and a tangible object in the tribal chiefs. Loyalty is a religion which is almost proof against its idol's selfishness and incompetence.

Caste is a symptom of arrested social development; and no community which tolerates it is free from the scourge of civil strife. Class war is the most salient fact in history. Warriors, termed Kshatriyas in Sanskrit, were the earliest caste. Under the law of specialisation defence fell to the lot of adventurous spirits, whose warlike prowess gave them unlimited prestige with the peaceful masses. They became the governing element, and were able to transmit their privileges by male filiation. But they had to reckon with the priests, descended from bards who attached themselves to the court of a Kshatriya prince and laid him under the spell of poetry. Lust of dominion is a manifestation of the Wish to Live; the priests used their tremendous power for selfish ends. They imitated the warriors in forming a caste, which claimed descent from Brahma, the Creator's head, while Kshatriyas represented his arms, and the productive classes his less noble members.

In the eleventh century B.C. the warrior clans rose in revolt against priestly arrogance: and Hindustan witnessed a conflict between the religious and secular arms. Brahminism had the terrors of hell fire on its side; feminine influence was its secret ally; the world is governed by brains, not muscles; and spiritual authority can defy the mailed fist. After a prolonged struggle the Kshatriyas were fain to acknowledge their inferiority.

When a hierocracy has been firmly established its evolution always follows similar lines. Ritual becomes increasingly elaborate: metaphysical dogma grows too subtle for a layman's comprehension. Commercialism spreads from the market to the sanctuary, whose guardians exploit the all-pervading fear of the unknown to serve their lust of luxury and rule.

Brahminism has never sought to win proselytes; the annals of ancient India record none of those atrocious persecutions which stained mediaeval Christianity. It competed with rival creeds by offering superior advantages: and the barbarous princes of India were kept under the priestly heel by an appeal to their animal instincts. A fungoid literature of abominations grew up in the Tantras, which are filthy dialogues between Siva, the destroying influence in nature, and his consorts. One of these, Káli by name, is the impersonation of slaughter. Her shrine, near Calcutta, is knee-deep in blood, and the *Dhyán* or formula for contemplating her glories, is a tissue of unspeakable obscenity. Most Hindus are Saktas, or worshippers of the female generative principle: happily for civilisation they are morally in advance of their creed. But it is a significant fact that Káli is the tutelary goddess of extremist politicians, whose minds are prepared for the acceptance of anarchism by the ever-present ideal of destruction.

It was Bengal's misfortune that its people received Brahminism in a corrupt and degenerate form. According to legend, King Adisur, who reigned there in the ninth century of our era, imported five priests from Kanauj to perform indispensable sacrifices. From this stock the majority of Bengali Brahmins claim descent. The immigrants were attended by five servants, who are the reputed ancestors of the Kayasth caste. In Sanskrit this word means "Standing on the Body," whence Kayasths claim to be Kshatriyas. But the tradition of a servile origin persisted, and they were forbidden to study the sacred writings. An inherited bent for literature has stood them in good stead: they became adepts in Persian, and English is almost their second mother-tongue to-day. Kayasths figure largely in Mr. Banerjea's tales: their history proves that the pen is mightier than the sword.

Economic necessity was the cause of the first invasion of India: the second was inspired by religion. The evolution of organised creeds is not from simple to complex, but *vice versa*. From the bed-rock of magic they rise through nature-worship and man-worship to monotheism. The god of a conquering tribe is imposed on subdued enemies, and becomes Lord of Heaven and Earth. Monotheism of this type took root among the Hebrews, from whom Mohammed borrowed the conception. His gospel was essentially militant and proselytising. Nothing can resist a blend of the aesthetic and combative instincts; within a century of the founder's death his successors had conquered Central Asia, and gained a permanent footing in Europe. In the tenth century a horde of Afghan Moslems penetrated Upper India.

The Kshatriya princes fought with dauntless courage, but unity of action was impossible; for the Brahmins fomented mutual jealousies and checked the growth of national spirit. They were subdued piecemeal; and in 1176 A.D. an Afghan Emperor governed Upper India from Delhi. The Aryan element in Bengal had lost its martial qualities; and offered no resistance to Afghan conquest, which was consummated in 1203. The invaders imposed their religion by fire and sword. The Mohammadans of Eastern Bengal, numbering 58 per cent. of the population, represent compulsory conversions effected between the thirteenth and seventeenth centuries. Eight hundred years of close contact have abated religious hatred; and occasional outbursts are due to priestly instigation. Hindus borrowed the Zenana system from their conquerors, who imitated them in discouraging widow-remarriages. Caste digs a gulf between followers of the rival creeds, but Mr. Banerjea's tales prove that a good understanding is possible. It is now imperilled by the curse of political agitation.

In 1526 the Afghan dynasty was subverted by a Mongol chieftain lineally descended from Tamerlane. His grandson Akbar's reign (1560–1605) was India's golden age. Akbar the Great was a ruler of the best modern type, who gave his subjects all the essentials of civilisation. But he knew that material prosperity is only the means to an end. Man, said Ruskin, is an engine whose motive power is the soul; and its fuel is love. Akbar called all the best elements in society to his side and linked them in the bonds of sympathy.

Religion in its highest phase is coloured by mysticism which seeks emblems of the hidden source of harmony in every form of life. Anthropomorphic conceptions are laid aside; ritual is abandoned as savouring of magic; hierocracy as part of an obsolete caste system; metaphysical dogma because the Infinite cannot be weighed in the balances of human reason. The truce to fanaticism called by Akbar the Great encouraged a poet and reformer named Tulsi Dása (1532–1623) to point a surer way to salvation. He adored Krishna, the preserving influence incarnate as Ráma, and rehandled Valmiki's great epic, the Rámáyana, in the faint rays of Christian light which penetrated India during that age of transition. Buddha had proclaimed the brotherhood of man; Tulsi Dása deduced it from the fatherhood of God. The Preserver, having sojourned among men, can understand their infirmities, and is ever ready to save his sinful creatures who call upon him. The duty of leading others to the fold is imposed on believers, for we are all children of the same Father. Tulsi Dása's Rámáyana is better known in Bihar and the United Provinces than is the Bible in rural England. The people of Hindustan are not swayed by relentless fate, nor by the goddess of destruction. Their prayers are addressed to a God who loves his meanest adorer; they accept this world's buffetings with resignation: while Ráma reigns all is well.

If the hereditary principle were sound, the Empire cemented together by Akbar's statecraft might have defied aggression. His successors were debauchees or fanatics. They neglected the army; a recrudescence of the nomad instinct sent them wandering over India with a locust-like horde of followers; Hindus were persecuted, and their temples were destroyed. So the military castes whose religion was threatened, rose in revolt; Viceroys threw off allegiance, and carved out kingdoms for themselves. Within a century of Akbar's death his Empire was a prey to anarchy.

India had hitherto enjoyed long spells of immunity from foreign interference. Her people, defended by the Himalayan wall and the ocean, were free to develop their own scheme of national life; and world-forces which pierce the thickest crust of custom, reached them in attenuated volume. Their isolation ended when the sea was no longer a barrier; and for maritime nations it is but an extension of their territory. A third invasion began in the sixteenth century, and has continued till our own day. The underlying motive was not economic necessity, nor religious enthusiasm, but sheer lust of gain.

In 1498 Vasco da Gama discovered an all-sea route to India, thus opening the fabulous riches of Asia to hungry Europe. Portuguese, Dutch, French and English adventurers embarked in a struggle for Indian commerce, in which our ancestors were victorious because they obtained the command of the sea, and had the whole resources of the mother-country at their back.

Westerners are so imbued with the profit-making instinct that they mentally open a ledger account in order to prove that India gains more than she loses by dependence on the people of these islands. It cannot be denied that the fabric of English administration is a noble monument of the civil skill and military prowess developed by our race. We have given the peninsula railways and canals, postal and telegraph systems, a code of laws which is far in advance of our own. Profound peace broods over the empire, famine and pestilence are fought with the weapons of science. It would be easy to pile up items on the debit side of our imaginary cash-book. Free trade has destroyed indigenous crafts wholesale, and quartered the castes who pursued them on an over-taxed soil. Incalculable is the waste of human life and inherited skill caused by the shifting of productive energy from India to Great Britain, Germany and America. It cannot be said that the oversea commerce, which amounted in 1907–8 to £241,000,000, is an unmixed benefit. The empire exports food and raw materials, robbing the soil of priceless constituents, and buys manufactured goods which ought to be produced at home. Foreign commerce is stimulated by the home charges, which average £18,000,000, and it received an indirect bounty by the closure of the mints in 1893. The textile industry of Lancashire was built upon a prohibition of Indian muslins: it now exports yarn and piece goods to the tune of £32,000,000, and this trade was unjustly favoured at the expense of local mills under the Customs Tariff of 1895. But there are forces in play for good or evil which cannot be appraised in money. From a material point of view our Government is the best and most honest in existence. If it fails to satisfy the psychical cravings of India there are shortcomings on both sides; and some of them are revealed by Mr. Banerjea's tales.

Caste.—As a *Kulin*, or pedigreed Brahmin, he is naturally prone to magnify the prestige of his order. It has been sapped by incidents of foreign rule and the spread of mysticism. Pandits find their stupendous lore of less account than the literary baggage of a university graduate. Brahmin pride is outraged by the advancement of men belonging to inferior castes. The priesthood's dream is to regain the ascendancy usurped by a race of *Mlecchas* (barbarians); and it keeps orthodox Hindus in a state of suppressed revolt. One centre of the insidious agitation is the fell goddess Káli's shrine near Calcutta; another is Puna, which has for centuries been a stronghold of the clannish Máráthá Brahmans. Railways have given a mighty impetus to religion by facilitating access to places of pilgrimage; the post office keeps disaffected elements in touch; and English has become a *lingua franca.*

While Brahminism, if it dared, could proclaim a religious war, it has powerful enemies within the hierarchy. A desire for social recognition is universal. It was the Patricians' refusal to intermarry with Plebeians that caused the great constitutional struggles of Ancient Rome. Many of the lowest castes are rebelling against Brahmin arrogance. They have waxed rich by growing lucrative staples, and a strong minority are highly educated. Mystical sects have already thrown off the priestly yoke. But caste is by no means confined to races of Indian blood. What is the snobbery which degrades our English character but the Indo-German Sudra's reverence for his Brahmin? The Europeans constitute a caste which possesses some solidarity against "natives," and they have spontaneously adopted these anti-social distinctions. At the apex stand covenanted civilians; whose service is now practically a close preserve for white men. It is split into the Secretariat, who enjoy a superb climate *plus* Indian pay and furlough, and the "rank and file" doomed to swelter in the plains. *Esprit de corps,* which is the life-blood of caste, has vanished. Officers of the Educational Service, recruited from the same social strata, rank as "uncovenanted"; and a sense of humiliation reacts on their teaching.

The Land.—In 1765 Clive secured for the East India Company the right of levying land-tax in Bengal. It was then collected by zemindars, a few of whom were semi-independent nobles, and the rest mere farmers of revenue, who bid against one another at the periodical settlements. Tenant right apart, the conception of private property in the soil was inconceivable to the Indian mind. Every one knows that it was borrowed by English lawyers from the Roman codes, when commercialism destroyed the old feudal nexus. Lord Cornwallis's permanent Settlement of 1793 was a revolution as drastic in its degree as that which France was undergoing. Zemindars were presented with the land for which they had been mere rakers-in of revenue. It was parcelled out into "estates," which might be bought and sold like moveable property. A tax levied at customary rates became "rent" arrived at by a process of bargaining between the landlord and ignorant rustics. The Government demand was fixed for ever, but no attempt was made to safeguard the ryot's interests. Cornwallis and his henchmen fondly supposed that they were manufacturing magnates of the English type, who had made our agriculture a model for the world. They were grievously mistaken. Under the cast-iron law of sale most of the original zemindars lost their estates, which passed into the hands of parvenus saturated with commercialism. Bengal is not indebted to its zemindars for any of the new staples which have created so vast a volume of wealth. They are content to be annuitants on the land, and sub-infeudation has gone to incredible lengths. Most of them are absentees whose one thought is to secure a maximum of unearned increment from tillers of the soil. In 1765 the land revenue amounted to £3,400,000, of which £258,000 was allotted to zemindars. A century afterwards their net profits were estimated at £12,000,000, and they are now probably half as much again. The horrible oppression described by Mr. Banerjea is impossible in our era of law-courts, railways and newspapers. But it is always dangerous to bring the sense of brotherhood, on which civilisation depends, into conflict with crude animal instincts. In days of American slavery the planter's interest prompted him to treat his human cattle with consideration, yet Simon Legrees were not unknown. It is a fact that certain zemindars are in the habit of remeasuring their ryots' holdings periodically, and always finding more land than was set forth in the lease.

The Police.—A pale copy of Sir Robert Peel's famous system was introduced in 1861, when hosts of inspectors, sub-inspectors and head constables were let loose on Bengal. The new force was highly unpopular, and failed to attract the educated classes. Subaltern officers, therefore, used power for private ends, while the masses were so inured to oppression that they offered no resistance. There has been a marked improvement in the *personnel* of late years; and Mr. Banerjea's lurid pictures of corruption and petty tyranny apply to a past generation of policemen. The Lieutenant-Governor of Eastern Bengal does justice to a much-abused service in his Administrative Report for 1907–8. His Honour "believes the force to be a hard-working body of Government servants, the difficulties, trials, and even dangers of whose duties it is impossible for the public at large really to appreciate". He acknowledges that "India is passing through a period of transition. Old pre-possessions and unscientific methods must be cast aside, and the value of the confession must be held at a discount." Bengal policemen fail as egregiously as their British colleagues in coping with professional crime. Burglary is a positive scourge, and the habit of organising gang-robberies has spread to youths of the middle class.

Education.—Though Mr. Banerjea has no experience of the inner working of our Government offices, he speaks on education with an expert's authority. Lord Macaulay, who went to India in 1834 as legal member of Council, was responsible for the introduction of English as the vehicle of instruction. He had gained admission to the caste of Whigs, whose battle-cry was "Knowledge for the People," and his brilliant rhetoric overpowered the arguments of champions of oriental learning. Every one with a smattering of Sanskrit, Arabic or Persian, regrets the fact that those glorious languages have not been adequately cultivated in modern India. Bengali is a true daughter of the Sanskrit; it has Italian sweetness and German capacity for expressing abstract ideas. No degree of proficiency in an alien tongue can compensate for the neglect of the vernacular. Moreover, the curriculum introduced in the "thirties" was purely academic. It came to India directly from English universities, which had stuck fast in the ruts of the Renaissance. Undue weight was given to literary training, while science and technical skill were despised. Our colleges and schools do not attempt to build character on a foundation of useful habits and tastes that sweeten life; to ennoble ideals, or inspire self-knowledge, self-reliance, and self-control. Technical education is still in its infancy; and the aesthetic instinct which lies dormant in every Aryan's brain is unawakened. A race which invented the loom now invents nothing but grievances. In 1901 Bengal possessed 69,000 schools and colleges, attended by 1,700,000 pupils, yet only one adult male in 10 and one female in 144 can read and write! The Calcutta University is an examining body on the London model. It does not attempt to enforce discipline in a city which flaunts every vice known to great seaports and commercial centres, unmitigated by the social instinct. Nor is the training of covenanted civilians more satisfactory. In 1909 only 1 out of 50 selected candidates presented himself for examination in Sanskrit or Arabic! Men go out to India at twenty-four, knowing little of the ethnology, languages or history of the races they are about to govern.

Agriculture.—Seventy-two per cent. of the Bengalis live by cultivating the soil. The vast majority are in the clutches of some local Shylock, who sweeps their produce into his garners, doling out inadequate supplies of food and seed grain. Our courts of law are used by these harpies as engines of oppression; toil as he may the ryot is never free from debt. The current rates of interest leave no profit from agriculture or trade. Twelve to 18 per cent. is charged for loans on ample landed security; and ordinary cultivators are mulcted in 40 to 60. A haunting fear of civil discord, and purblind conservatism in the commercial castes, are responsible for the dearth of capital. India imports bullion amounting to £25,000,000 a year, to the great detriment of European credit, and nine-tenths of it is hoarded in the shape of ornaments or invested in land, which is a badge of social rank. Yet the Aryan nature is peculiarly adapted to co-operation. If facilities for borrowing at remunerative rates existed in towns, agricultural banks on the Schulze-Delitzsch and Raiffeisen systems would soon overspread the land. Credit and co-operative groupings for the purchase of seed, fertilisers and implements, are the twin pillars of rural industry. Indian ryots are quite as receptive of new ideas as English farmers. They bought many thousands of little iron sugar mills, placed on the market a generation back by some English speculators, and will adopt any improvements of practical value if the price is brought within their slender means.

The revolution which began a decade ago in America has not spread to Bengal, where the average yield of grain per acre is only 10 bushels as compared with 30 in Europe. Yet it has been calculated that another bushel would defray the whole cost of Government! Bengalis obey the injunction "increase and multiply" without regard for consequences. Their habitat has a population of 552 per square mile, and in some districts the ratio exceeds 900. Clearly there is a pressing need of scientific agriculture, to replace or supplement the rule-of-thumb methods in which the ryot is a past master.

The Bengali Character.—Mr. Banerjea has lifted a corner of the veil that guards the Indian's home from prying eyes. He shows that Bengalis are men of like passions with us. The picture is perhaps overcharged with shade. Sycophants, hustlers and cheats abound in every community; happily for the future of civilisation there is also a leaven of true nobility: "The flesh striveth against the spirit," nor does it always gain mastery. Having mixed with all classes for twenty eventful years, and speaking the vernacular fluently, I am perhaps entitled to hold an opinion on this much-vexed question. The most salient feature in the Indian nature is its boundless charity. There are no poor laws, and the struggle for life is very severe; yet the aged and infirm, the widow and the orphan have their allotted share in the earnings of every household. It is a symptom of approaching famine that beggars are perforce refused their daily dole. Cruelty to children is quite unknown. Parents will deny themselves food in order to defray a son's schooling-fees or marry a daughter with suitable provision. Bengalis are remarkably clannish: they will toil and plot to advance the interests of anyone remotely connected with them by ties of blood.

Their faults are the outcome of superstition, slavery to custom, and an unhealthy climate. Among them is a lack of moral courage, a tendency to lean on stronger natures, and to flatter a superior by feigning to agree with him. The standard of truth and honesty is that of all races which have been ground under heel for ages: deceit is the weapon of weaklings and slaves. Perjury has become a fine art, because our legal system fosters the chicane which is innate in quick-witted peoples. The same man who lies unblushingly in an English court, will tell the truth to an assembly of caste-fellows, or to the *Panchayat* (a committee of five which arbitrates in private disputes). Let British Pharisees study the working of their own Divorce and County Courts: they will not find much evidence of superior virtue! As for honesty, the essence of commercialism is "taking advantage of other people's needs," and no legal code has yet succeeded in drawing a line between fair and unfair trade. In India and Japan merchants are an inferior class; and loss of self-respect reacts unfavourably on the moral sense. Ingratitude is a vice attributed to Bengalis by people who have done little or nothing to elicit the corresponding virtue. As a matter of fact their memory is extremely retentive of favours. They will overlook any shortcomings in a ruler who has the divine gift of sympathy, and serve him with devotion. Macaulay has branded them with cowardice. If the charge were true, it was surely illogical and unmanly to reproach a community numbering 50,000,000 for inherited defects. Difference of environment and social customs will account for the superior virility of Europeans as compared with their distant kinsmen whose lot is cast in the sweltering tropics. But no one who has observed Bengali schoolboys standing up bare-legged to fast bowling will question their bravery. In fact, the instinct of combativeness is universal, and among protected communities it finds vent in litigation.

Englishmen who seek to do their duty by India have potential allies in the educated classes, who have grafted Western learning on a civilisation much more ancient than their own. Bengal has given many illustrious sons to the empire. Among the dead I may mention Pandits Ishwar Chandra Vidyasagar and Kissari Mohan Ganguli, whose vast learning was eclipsed by their zeal for social service; Dr. Sambhu Chandra Mukharji, whose biography I wrote in 1895; and Mr. Umesh Chandra Banarji, a lawyer who held his own with the flower of our English bar. A Bengali Brahmin is still with us who directs one of the greatest contracting firms in the empire. How much brighter would India's outlook be if this highly-gifted race were linked in bonds of sympathy with our own!

The women of the Gangetic delta deserve a better fate than is assigned to them by Hindu and Mohammadan custom. They are kept in leading-strings from the cradle to the grave; their intellect is rarely cultivated, their affections suffer atrophy from constant repression. Yet Mr. Banerjea draws more than one picture of wifely devotion, and the instinctive good sense which is one of the secrets of feminine influence. Women seldom fail to rise to the occasion when opportunity is vouchsafed them. The late Maharani Surnomoyi of Cossimbazar managed her enormous estates with acumen; and her charities were as lavish as Lady Burdett-Coutts's. Toru Dutt, who died in girlhood, wrote French and English verses full of haunting sweetness. It is a little premature for extremists to prate of autonomy while their women are prisoners or drudges.

Superstition.—Modes of thought surviving from past ages of intellectual growth are the chief obstacles in the path of progress. Mr. Banerjea's tales contain many references to magic—a pseudo-science which clings to the world's religions and social polity. It is doubtful whether the most civilised of us has quite shaken off the notion that mysterious virtues may be transmitted without the impetus of will-power. Latin races are haunted by dread of the Evil Eye; advertisements of palmists, astrologers and crystal-gazers fill columns of our newspapers. Rational education alone enables us to trace the sequence of cause and effect which is visible in every form of energy. Until this truth is generally recognised no community can eradicate the vices of superstition.

The "unrest" of which we hear so much finds no echo in Mr. Banerjea's pages. It is, indeed, confined to a minute percentage of the population, even including the callow schoolboys who have been tempted to waste precious years on politics. The masses are too ignorant and too absorbed by the struggle for existence to care one jot for reforms. They may, however, be stirred to blind fury by appealing to their prejudices. Therein lies a real danger. Divergence of religious ideals, to which I have already alluded, accounts for the tranquillity that prevails throughout Bihar as compared with the spirit of revolution in Bengal proper. The microbe of anarchy finds an excellent culture-ground in minds which grovel before the goddess Káli. But the unrest cannot be isolated from other manifestations of cosmic energy, which flash from mind to mind and keep the world in turmoil. Every force of nature tends to be periodic. The heart's systole and diastole; alternations of day and night, of season and tide, are reflected in the history of our race. Progress is secured by the swing of a giant pendulum from East to West, the end of each beat ushering in drastic changes in religion, economics and social polity. It is probable that one of these cataclysmic epochs opened with the victories wrested from Russia by Japan. The democratic upheaval which began five hundred years ago is assuming Protean forces; and amongst them is the malady aptly styled "constitutionalitis" by Dr. Dillon. The situation in India demands prescience and statecraft. Though world-forces cannot be withstood, they are susceptible of control by enlightened will-power. Will peace be restored by the gift of constitutional government at a crisis when the august Mother of Parliaments is herself a prey to faction?

It is worthy of note that the self-same spirit has always been rife in Bengal, where every village has its *Dals*—local Montagues and Capulets, whose bickerings are a fertile source of litigation.

Mr. Banerjea's tales were written for his own countrymen, and needed extensive revision in order to render them intelligible to Western readers. I have preserved the author's spirit and phraseology; and venture to hope that this little book will shed some light on the problem of Indian administration.

FRANCIS H. SKRINE.

THE PRIDE OF KADAMPUR.

Kadampur is a country village which is destitute of natural or artificial attractions and quite unknown to fame. Its census population is barely 1,500, four-fifths of whom are low-caste Hindus, engaged in cultivation and river-fishing; the rest Mohammadans, who follow the same avocations but dwell in a *Párá* (quarter) of their own. The *Bhadralok*, or Upper Crust, consists of two Brahman and ten Kayastha (writer-caste) families. Among the latter group Kumodini Kanta Basu's took an unquestioned lead. He had amassed a modest competence as sub-contractor in the Commissariat during the second Afghan War, and retired to enjoy it in his ancestral village. His first care was to rebuild the family residence, a congenial task which occupied five years and made a large hole in his savings. It slowly grew into a masonry structure divided into two distinct *Mahâls* (wings)—the first inhabited by men-folk; the second sacred to the ladies and their attendants. Behind it stood the kitchen; and the *Pujardálán* (family temple) occupied a conspicuous place in front, facing south. The usual range of brick cattle-sheds and servants' quarters made up quite an imposing group of buildings.

Villagers classed amongst the gentry are wont to gather daily at some *Chandimandap* (a rustic temple dedicated to the goddess Durga, attached to most better-class houses). Kumodini Babu's was a favourite rendezvous, and much time was killed there in conversation, card-playing, and chess. Among the group assembled, one crisp afternoon in February, was an old gentleman, called Shámsundar Ghosh, and known to hosts of friends as "Shám Babu". He was head clerk in a Calcutta merchant's office, drawing Rs. 60 a month (£48 a year at par), which sufficed for the support of his wife and a son and daughter, respectively named Susil and Shaibalini. After a vain attempt to make two ends meet in expensive Calcutta, he had settled down at the outskirts of Kadampur, which has a railway station within half an hour's run of the Metropolis. Shám Babu's position and character were generally respected by neighbours, who flocked to his house for Calcutta gossip.

On this particular occasion talk ran on Kadampur requirements, and somebody opined that another tank for bathing and drinking purposes ought to be excavated at once; he did not say by whom.

"True," observed Sham Babu, "but a market is still more necessary. We have to trudge four miles for our vegetables and fish, which are obtainable in a more or less stale condition only twice a week. If one were started here, it would be a great boon to ten villages at least." Kumodini Babu assented, without further remark, and the subject dropped.

It came up again on the following Sunday, when Kumodini Babu said to his friend:—

"I have been thinking about your idea of a market in this village, and should like, if possible, to establish one myself. How much would it cost me? As an old commissariat contractor, I am well up in the price of grain, fodder and *ghi* (clarified butter used in cooking), but I really know very little about other things."

The confession elicited a general laugh, and Shám Babu replied, "It will be a matter of Rs. 200".

"Two hundred rupees! Surely that is far too much for a range of huts."

"True enough. Your own bamboo clumps, straw-stacks and stores of cordage would provide raw material; and as for labour, all you have to do is to order some of your ryots (tenants) who are behindhand with their rent to work for you gratis."

"That would be contrary to my principles. How are these poor people to live while engaged in *begár* (forced labour) on my behalf? They must be paid."

"Very well, then, let us set apart Rs. 20 to meet the cost of market buildings. But, for the first few weeks, you will have to buy up the unsold stock of perishable goods brought by *Farias* (hucksters); you must patronise the shopkeepers who open stalls for selling grain, cloth, confectionery, tobacco and trinkets. Once these people find that they are making fair profits they will gladly pay you rent for space allotted, besides tolls on the usual scale. At least Rs. 180 must be set apart for these preliminary expenses."

Kumodini Babu never did anything in haste. A fortnight elapsed ere he announced to the neighbours gathered in his *Chandimandap* that he intended starting a bi-weekly market on a vacant plot measuring one *Bigha* (one-third of an acre), known as the Kamárbári (Anglice, "Abode of Blacksmiths"). On an auspicious day towards the end of April, he inaugurated the new enterprise with some ceremony. His own ryots were enjoined to attend; shopkeepers, hucksters, and fishermen who had hitherto gone much further afield, came in considerable numbers; and business was amazingly brisk. Zemindars (landed proprietors) generally have to wait for months and spend money like water before they gain a pice (a bronze coin worth a farthing) from a new market. Kumodini Babu, however, began to reap where he had sown in less than a fortnight. Not an inch of space in the Karmárbári remained unoccupied; his Hát-Gomastha, or bailiff, levied rent and tolls for vendors, at whose request the market was proclaimed a tri-weekly one. His fame as a man of energy and public spirit spread over ten villages, whose people felt that he was one who would give them good counsel in times of difficulty.

There is some truth in the notion that fortune's gifts seldom come singly. Kumodini Babu's success in a business venture was immediately followed by one in his domestic affairs. It fell out in this wise. Shám Babu's daughter, Shaibalini, was still unmarried, though nearly thirteen and beautiful enough to be the pride of Kadampur. Money was, indeed, the only qualification she lacked, and Sham Babu's comparative poverty kept eligible suitors at a distance. For three years he had sought far and wide for a son-in-law and was beginning to fear that he might, after all, be unable to fulfil the chief duty of a Hindu parent. One evening his wife unexpectedly entered the parlour where he was resting after a heavy day at office.

"Why has the moon risen so early?" he asked.

"Because the moon can't do otherwise," she answered, with a faint smile. "But, joking apart, I want to consult you about Saili. Our neighbour Kanto Babu's wife called on me just before you returned from Calcutta, and, after beating about the bush, suggested Kumodini Babu's younger son, Nalini, as a suitable match for her."

Shám Babu's face wore a worried look.

"Surely that would be flying too high for such as us," he rejoined. "The Basus are comparatively rich, and very proud of their family which settled here during the Mughal days (*i.e.*, before British rule, which in Bengal date from 1765). Young Nalini is reading for his B.A. examination and wants to be a pleader (advocate). Kumodini Babu would hardly allow his son to marry the daughter of a poor clerk."

"Still, there is no harm in trying," remarked the wife. "If you don't feel equal to approaching him, there's Kanto Babu who would do so. It was his wife who broached the subject to me, which makes me think that they have been discussing it together."

"An excellent idea," exclaimed Shám Babu. "I'll go to him at once." And taking his stick, he set out for Kanto Babu's house, which was barely fifty yards off. In half an hour he returned to gladden his wife with the news that their neighbour had consented to act as a go-between.

Kanto Babu was as good as his word. That very evening he called on Kumodini Babu, whom he found reading the *Mahábhárata* (an epic poem). After dwelling now on this matter, now on that, he asked casually:—

"Have you never thought of getting Nalini married? He is over twenty, I believe."

"My wife has been urging me to look out for a wife for him, but in my opinion he is too young for such responsibilities. Better wait till he has passed the B.A. examination."

"Your wife's idea is sounder than yours, if I may be permitted to say so. Just think of the awful temptations to which unmarried students are exposed in that sink of profligacy, Calcutta! How many promising lads have succumbed to them, wrecking their own lives and causing bitter grief to their parents!"

Kumodini Babu started. "You surprise me! I had no idea that Calcutta was as bad as you paint it. We must certainly get Nalini married at once. I wonder whether you know of a likely match for him. I don't care about money, but—"

"That I do," interrupted Kanto Babu, "There's Shám Babu's daughter, Shaibalini. What a pretty creature she is; modest, loving and kind-hearted! You won't find her equal in this *eláqa* (lit. jurisdiction). If you approve, I will gladly be your spokesman with her family."

Kumodini Babu mused awhile before answering. "I know Shaibalini well by reputation, and she is all you describe her. Shám Babu, too, comes of excellent lineage, though he is not a Zemindar, and depends on service. I should not object to marrying Nalini with his daughter. But wait a bit: what *gotra* (clan) does he belong to?"

"I believe he is a Dakhin Rárhi," answered Kanto Babu.

"But I am an Uttar Rárhi," remarked Kumodini Babu. "Is not that a fatal objection?"

For the benefit of non-Hindu readers I may explain that Kayasthas are split into clans—probably a survival of the tribal organisation which preceded the family almost everywhere. According to tradition, a King of Bengal named Ádisur imported five Brahmans, and as many Kayastha servants from Kanauj in Upper India. From the latter are descended the Ghosh, Basu, Mitra, Guha, and Datta families. The first four are generally recognised as Kúlin (Angl., "aristocratic") Kayasthas, while the Dattas and seven other families are known as Sindhu Maulik—"coming of a good stock". Ádisur and his companions found 700 Brahmans and the same number of Kayasthas already established in Bengal. These are the supposed ancestors of a large number of Kayastha families still termed Saptasati, "the Seven Hundred". The ancient Greeks reckoned their neighbours beyond the Hellenic pale as "barbarians". So Brahmans and Kayasthas of Central Bengal styled their congeners north of the Ganges *Rárh,* or "uncivilised". The epithet survives in Uttar (north) and Dakhin (south) Rárhi, but has lost its offensive meaning. Bárendra is another phrase for the inhabitants of a tract north of the Ganges, which answers to the modern districts of Rajshahi, Pabna, and Bogra.

Kanto Babu was evidently perplexed; but after reflecting for a short time he asked, "Now why should such a trifling matter cause any trouble whatever? The time has long since passed away when arbitrary difference of clan was considered a bar to marriage among Kayasthas."

"You are quite right," was Kumodini Babu's reply, "and personally I am above these old-fashioned prejudices. My daughter-in-law may be Dakhin Rárhi, Banga-ja, or Bárendri for all I care, provided she be comely, well-mannered and come of good stock. But will Shám Babu be equally tolerant?"

"That I can't say until I have consulted him," answered Kanto Babu. "One thing more I must know. What is your idea of *Dená Páona* (a word answering to our 'settlements')?"

"Rám, Rám!" exclaimed Kumodini Babu. "Am I the man to sell my son for filthy lucre? I hear that Calcutta folks occasionally do so, but I am quite opposed to the custom. Should Shám Babu agree to this match, I will make no stipulations whatever as to a money payment. He is in very moderate circumstances, and may give whatever he chooses. Please see him at once and let me have his decision."

Kanto Babu promised to do so and withdrew, inwardly chuckling over his diplomacy.

Shám Babu called on him the same evening to learn its issue. He was delighted to find that Kumodini Babu was not averse to the match, but his face fell on hearing of the difference of clan. Observing his agitation, Kanto Babu observed gently, "I don't see why a matter, which is not even mentioned in our Shástras (holy books), should cause one moment's hesitation. Pluck up your courage, man, and all will go well."

"Perhaps so," murmured Shám Babu. "But I do stand in awe of the Samáj" (a caste-assembly which pronounces excommunication for breaches of custom).

"That's all nonsense! Look at our friend Kunjalál Babu who has just married his son to a Bárendri girl. Is he an outcast? Certainly not. It is true that the ultra-orthodox kicked a bit at first; but they all came round, and joined in the ceremony with zest. I can quote scores of similar instances to prove that this prejudice against marrying into a different clan is quite out of date."

Shám Babu had nothing to urge in opposition to these weighty arguments. He promised to let Kanto Babu have a definite reply on the morrow and kept his word. Having endured a curtain lecture from his wife, who proved to him that an alliance with the Basu family offered advantages far outweighing the slight risk there was of excommunication, he authorised Kanto Babu to assure Kumodini Babu that the proposed match had his hearty approval. Once preliminaries were satisfactorily settled, all other arrangements proceeded apace. The Páká Dekhá is a solemn visit paid by males of the future bridegroom's family to that of his betrothed, during which they are feasted and decide all details regarding the marriage ceremonies. It passed off without a hitch, and the *purohit* (family priest) fixed Sraván 17th as an auspicious day for consummating the union. Thenceforward preparations were made for celebrating it in a manner worthy of the esteem in which both families were held.

Kumodini Babu issued invitations to all his relatives. Chief amongst these was a younger brother, Ghaneshyám Basu by name, who practised as a pleader (advocate) at Ghoria, where he had built a house after disposing of his interest in the family estate to Kumodini Babu. This important person was asked to supervise the ceremonies, inasmuch as Kumodini Babu's increasing age and infirmities rendered him unfit to do so efficiently, while his eldest son, yclept Jadu Babu, had barely reached man's estate. The letter of invitation referred incidentally to the difference of clan as a matter of no importance. Kumodini Babu's disappointment may be conceived when he got an answer from his younger brother, expressing strong disapproval of the match and ending with a threat to sever all connection with the family if it were persisted in! The recipient at first thought of running up to Ghoria, in view of softening Ghaneshyám Babu's heart by a personal appeal, but the anger caused by his want of brotherly feeling prevailed. Kumodini Babu and his wife agreed that matters had gone too far to admit of the marriage being broken off. If Ghaneshyám did not choose to take part in it, so much the worse for him!

Soon after dusk on Sraván 17th, Nalini entered his palanquin, arrayed in a beautiful costume of Benares silk. The wedding procession set out forthwith, amid a mighty blowing of conch-shells and beating of drums. At 8 P.M. it reached the bride's abode, where her family, with Shám Babu at the head, were ready to receive them. An hour later Nalini was conducted to the inner apartments, where the marriage ceremony began. It lasted until nearly eleven o'clock, when the young couple were taken to the Básárghar, or nuptial apartment. During these rites the men-folk were perhaps more pleasantly engaged in doing ample justice to a repast provided for them in the outer rooms. Then they chewed betels in blissful rumination, before separating with emphatic acknowledgments of the hospitality they had enjoyed.

On the following afternoon both bridegroom and bride were taken in palanquins to Kumodini Babu's house, where she instantaneously won every heart by her grace and beauty. Two days later the Bau-Bhát ceremony was held. This is a feast in the course of which the bride (*bau*) distributes cooked rice (*bhát*) with her own hands to bidden guests, in token of her reception into her husband's family and clan. Kumodini Babu had requisitioned an immense supply of dainties from local *goálas* (dairymen) and *moiras* (confectioners) with a view to eclipsing all previous festivals of the kind.

Early in the morning of the Bau-Bhát day a palanquin was carried into Kumodini Babu's courtyard; and who should emerge from it but Ghaneshyám Babu! He ran up to his brother, who was sitting with some neighbours in the parlour, and, clasping his feet, implored forgiveness. Kumodini Babu's heart leaped for joy. Tenderly did he embrace the penitent, who admitted that his peace of mind had fled from the moment he penned that cruel letter. He now saw the absurdity of his prejudices, and begged Kumodini Babu to forget his unbrotherly conduct. It is needless to add that the prayer was cordially granted and that Ghaneshyám Babu received a blessing from his elder brother. Thanks to his supervision the Bau-Bhát feast passed off at night without the slightest contretemps. Ten years later people still dwelt on the magnificent hospitality they had received, and held Kumodini Babu up as a model to fathers-in-law. In order that all classes might rejoice with him, he remitted a year's rent to every ryot, besides lavishing considerable sums on Brahmans and poor folk. The more enlightened section of Kayasthas were unanimous in pronouncing him to be a true Hindu, on whose descendants the gods on high would pour down their choicest blessings. There were others, however, whose malignity found material to work on in his disregard of caste prejudices.

THE RIVAL MARKETS.

The immediate success of Kumodini Babu's market caused infinite annoyance to Ramani Babu, who owned one long established in the neighbourhood. Hucksters and country-folk found the tolls levied there so much lighter, that the attendance at Ramani's fell off grievously. It is well known that when a new market is started, proprietors already in the field endeavour to break it up with the aid of paid *láthiáls* (clubmen). If, as often happens, the daring speculator be a man of substance, he employs similar means in his defence. Free fights occur on market-days, ending in many a broken head—sometimes in slaughter. The battle is directed by Gomasthas (bailiffs) on either side, with the full knowledge of their masters, who keep discreetly aloof from the fray.

Ramani Babu did not foresee that his property would be injured by the new venture, and allowed it to be firmly established without striking a single blow. Finding a lamentable decrease in his receipts, he ordered the bailiff to "go ahead," and took an early train for Calcutta in order to set up an alibi in case of legal proceedings. A day or two later his bailiff, attended by six or seven men armed with iron-shod bamboo staves, assembled at the outskirts of Kumodini Babu's market, on a spot where four roads met.

Ere long a cart was descried approaching from eastwards, whose driver bawled snatches of song and puffed his hookah between whiles. When it reached the crossing, the bailiff shouted:—

"Stop! whither so early, friend?"

"To market," the man replied carelessly.

"Whose market?"

"The new one, started by Kumodini Babu."

"What have you got in those baskets of yours?"

"Oh, sweet potatoes, *brinjáls* (egg-plants), and a lot of other vegetables."

"Why don't you attend Ramani Babu's market?"

"Because it does not pay me to go there."

"So you used to take your vegetables to Ramani Babu's market?"

"Yes; but there are hardly any customers left. Now please let me go; the sun is high up."

"So you won't obey me!"

"No!" roared the carter, prodding his oxen viciously.

"Stop a minute, I tell you! Whose ryot (tenant) are you?"

"Ramani Babu's."

"What, you are his ryot and yet are acting against his interests? If he hears of your perfidy he will certainly turn you out of his estate!"

"Why should he?" asked the fellow, now thoroughly frightened. "I am a very poor man, and Ramani Babu is my father and mother. He cannot object to my selling a few vegetables wherever I please."

"But he does object," rejoined the bailiff sternly. "What's your name and residence?"

"Sádhu Sheikh, of Simulgachi."

"Now, do you know who I am?"

"No-o," replied Sádhu, hesitatingly.

"I am Ramani Babu's new bailiff, sent with these men to see that his market is well attended."

Sádhu's tone completely changed. "Salám, Babu," he whined. "I did not know who you were. Please let me pass or I shall be too late."

"Not so fast, friend," shouted the bailiff. "Once for all, are you going to obey me or not?"

Sádhu prodded his bullocks into a lumbering canter; but the bailiff gave a signal to his clubmen, who ran after him, dragged him out of the cart, and thrashed him soundly. Then two of them escorted him, with his wares, to their master's market, which was being held about three miles away. The bailiff waited at the crossing for new arrivals. They were not long in coming. A fishwoman, heavily laden, passed by. He hailed her, and on learning whither she was bound, ordered his men to drag her to their master's market, which they did, despite the volume of abuse which she hurled at their heads. In this manner some half a dozen deserters were captured and escorted to the old market.

The story of his tyranny spread like wildfire through neighbouring villages, with many amplifications, of course. Kumodini Babu heard that his rival had arrested a hundred frequenters of his market and was about to destroy the shelters he had erected for salesmen. This information filled him with anxiety and, after consulting friends, he lodged a complaint at the police station. In the remote interior of Bengal policemen are all-powerful. They usurp authority to which they are not entitled by law, and use it for private ends. All classes go in perpetual fear of them; for, by a stroke of the pen, they can ruin reputations and defeat justice. No one has recourse to their dreaded agency who can avoid doing so or has the means of gratifying their greed. By giving a handsome *douceur* to the Sub-Inspector, Kumodini Babu obtained a promise of support, which he was simple enough to rely upon.

Meantime Ramani Babu's market bailiff was not idle. Knowing that he had acted illegally, he resolved to "square" the executive. So, one evening, he persuaded his master to accompany him to the police station, provided with a bundle of ten-rupee currency notes. After discussing commonplaces with the Sub-Inspector, they adjourned to an inner room, where they induced him to take their side—for very weighty reasons.

Matters now began to look ugly for Kumodini Babu. Every vendor who approached his market was intercepted. He implored the help of the Sub-Inspector, who, however, observed a strict neutrality, hinting that the complainant was at liberty to defend himself with the aid of clubmen. But Kumodini Babu was a man of peace, and finding the policeman something less than lukewarm, he resigned himself to the inevitable.

His evil star continued to prevail, for, soon after these untoward events, it brought him into collision with the police. In consequence of an understanding with Ramani Babu, the Sub-Inspector took to buying provisions from the few shopkeepers who still attended Kumodini Babu's market and referring them to him for payment. His constables, too, helped themselves freely to rice and vegetables without even asking the price, and had their shoes blacked gratis by Kumodini Babu's *muchis* (leather-dressers). His bailiff put up with their vagaries, until the shopkeepers came in a body to say that unless they were stopped, the market would be entirely deserted. The luckless Zemindar was staggered by the tale of oppression. He paid for every article extorted by the police, but strictly forbade the vendors to give any further credit. The Sub-Inspector was deeply incensed in finding this source of illicit profit cut off, and his vengeance was perpetrated under the pretence of law.

One evening, while Kumodini Babu was conning the *Mahábhárata* (an ancient epic) in his parlour, the Sub-Inspector came in, armed with a search warrant issued by the Deputy Magistrate of Ghoria, which he showed the astonished master of the house. A charge of receiving stolen property brought against him was indeed a bolt from the blue; but when Kumodini Babu regained his scattered wits, he told the Sub-Inspector scornfully that he might search every hole and corner of his house. For half an hour the police were occupied in turning his furniture and boxes topsy-turvy; and at last the Sub-Inspector went alone into a lumber-room, while his head constable kept Kumodini's attention fixed on the contents of an *almeira* (ward-robe) which he was searching. Shouting, "I have found the property!" he emerged from the room with a box containing various articles of gold and silver, which he said were hidden under some straw. On comparing them with a list in his possession he declared that they exactly tallied with property reported as part of the spoils of a burglary in the neighbouring village. In vain Kumodini Babu protested his entire innocence and asked whether he, a respectable Zemindar, was likely to be a receiver of stolen goods. He was handcuffed and taken to the police station on foot, while the Sub-Inspector followed in a palanquin. Kumodini Babu's women-folk filled the house with their lamentations; and his eldest son, Jadu Náth, was the first to recover from the prostration caused by sudden misfortune. He had a pony saddled and galloped to the railway station, whence he telegraphed to his uncle, Ghaneshyám Babu, the pleader, "Father arrested: charge receiving stolen goods". Ghaneshyám arrived by the next train, and after hearing the facts returned to Ghoria, where he applied to the Deputy Magistrate for bail. There was a strong disinclination to grant it, owing to the gravity of the charge; but finally an order was issued, releasing the prisoner on personal recognisance of Rs. 10,000 and two sureties of Rs. 5,000. The necessary security was immediately forthcoming, and Kumodini Babu found himself temporarily a free man, after enduring nearly forty-eight hours of unspeakable misery in the station lock-up.

In due course his case came on for hearing before the Deputy Magistrate. Ghaneshyám Babu secured the services of a fighting member of the Calcutta bar and was indefatigable in his efforts to unearth the nefarious plot against his brother. Proceedings lasted for four days in a court packed with spectators. The Sub-Inspector and his accomplices told their story speciously enough. A burglary had really been committed and the jewellery found in Kumodini Babu's outhouse was proved to have been part of the stolen goods. The issue was—who placed them there? On this point the Sub-Inspector's evidence was not by any means satisfactory. He finally broke down under rigorous cross-examination, and was forced to admit that it was quite possible that some one acting on his behalf had hidden the property in Kumodini Babu's lumber-room. The battle of the markets was related in all its dramatic details. Shopkeepers and ryots alike, seeing that justice was likely to prevail, came forward to depose to acts of tyranny by Ramani Babu's servants and their allies, the police. Evidence of the prisoner's high character was forthcoming, while his age and dignified bearing spoke strongly in his favour. The Magistrate saw that he had been the victim of an abominable conspiracy and released him amid the suppressed plaudits of the audience. His reasons for discharge contained severe strictures on the local police, and even suggested their prosecution. Thus, after weeks of agonising suspense and an expenditure on legal fees running into thousands of rupees, Kumodini Babu was declared innocent. He took the humiliation so much to heart, that he meditated retiring to that refuge for storm-tossed souls, Benares. But Ghaneshyám Babu strongly dissuaded him from abandoning the struggle, at least until he had turned the tables on his enemies. So Kumodini Babu moved the District Magistrate to issue process against Ramani Babu and the Sub-Inspector. He met with a refusal, however, probably because the higher authorities thought fit to hush up a glaring scandal which might "get into the papers," and discredit the administration. Ramani Babu, therefore, was not molested, but his accomplice was departmentally censured, and transferred to an unhealthy district. Kumodini Babu also thought of discontinuing the market which had been the fount and origin of his misfortunes. Here again his brother objected that such a course would be taken to indicate weakness and encourage further attacks. His advice was followed. The new market throve amazingly, while Ramani Babu's was quite deserted.

A FOUL CONSPIRACY.

On a certain morning in February Ramani Babu sprung a mine on his tenants by circulating a notice among them to the effect that they would have to pay up every pice of rent on or before the 10th prox. Some hastened to discharge their liabilities, while others ran about asking for loans or sat with downcast eyes, unable to decide what course to take. The English reader is perhaps unaware that every Bengal landowner is required to pay revenue to Government four times a year, *viz.*, on the 28th January, March, June and September. Any one failing to do so before sunset on these dates becomes a defaulter, and his estate is put up to auction in order to satisfy the demand, however small it may be. Property worth many thousands of rupees has often been sold for arrears of eight annas (a shilling) or even less. The near approach of these *kist* (rent) days is of course a period of great anxiety to landlords; some of whom are forced to borrow the necessary amount on the security of their wives' ornaments.

On March 28th, 18—, Ramani Babu had to pay about Rs. 10,000 as land revenue; but his ryots' crops had failed, owing to want of rain, and by the end of February he had been able to realise only Rs. 1,000, the greater portion by threats of force. The Indian peasant's lot is not a happy one. He depends solely on the produce of the soil, which yields little or nothing if the annual rains should fail, or there be an excess of moisture. Millions of cultivators never know what it is to have a good, solid meal. In order to meet the landlord's demands they have recourse to a *Maháјan* (moneylender) whose exactions leave them a slender margin for subsistence. But religion and ages of slavery render them submissive creatures. They murmur only when very hard pressed.

Sádhu Sheikh, of Simulgachi, lived by raising vegetables for sale in Kumodini Babu's market, until he was forbidden to do so by Ramani Babu's clubmen. Failing this resource, he abandoned the little trade; and thus got deeper into the books of his moneylender. At this crisis he received a written notice ordering him to attend Ramani Babu's *kacheri* (office) on 17th March without fail. A visit to the local moneylender was fruitless and only led to a hint that old scores must be cleared off. So Sádhu returned home crestfallen and determined to abide by his fate. On obeying the summons, he found Ramani Babu sitting in his office to receive rent, which was brought him by a crowd of dejected-looking ryots. A great hubbub was going on; one Bemani insisting that he had paid up to date while Ramani Babu's *gomastha* (bailiff) stoutly denied the assertion and called on the objector to produce his receipt. This was not forthcoming for the simple reason that Bemani had mislaid it. He asked the bailiff to show him the ledger account, and after spelling through the items laboriously be found that not a pice stood to his credit, although he had paid nearly sixty rupees since the last *kist* (rent) day. There are few who understand the value of the *dákhilas* (rent receipts) which landlords are compelled by law to give them. The little slips of paper are lost or destroyed, with the result that many ryots have had to pay twice over. Bemani vainly invoked Allah to witness that he had discharged his dues; the bailiff ordered him to pay within twenty-four hours on pain of severe punishment. Goaded to fury by this palpable injustice the poor man declined to do anything of the kind. At this stage Ramani Babu intervened:—

"You son of a pig, are you going to obey my orders or not?"

"No, I have paid once, and I won't pay again," yelled Bemani, thoroughly roused.

Ramani Babu beckoned to a stalwart doorkeeper from the Upper Provinces, who was standing near.

"Sarbeshwar, give this rascal a taste of your Shámchand (cane)!"

He was zealously obeyed and poor Bemani was thrashed until he lay writhing in agony on the ground. After taking his punishment he rose, and looking defiantly at Ramani Babu said:—

"You have treated me cruelly; but you will find that there is a God who watches all our actions. He will certainly deal out retribution to you!" He then turned to go.

"I see you are not yet cured," exclaimed Ramani Babu. "Let him have another dose of Shámchand."

"Yes, go on!" roared Bemani, "beat me as much as you please; you'll have reason to repent sooner or later!" With this remark he stood erect, looking fearlessly at his tormentors. Sarbeshwar administered another welting, which drew blood at every stroke but was borne without sound or movement. When the doorkeeper stopped for want of breath, Bemani cast a look of scorn at Ramani Babu and strode out of the house in silence, full of rage.

Presently another disturbance was heard. One of the ryots had paid his rent in full but declined to add the usual commission exacted by the bailiffs, who fell on him in a body and pummelled him severely.

Sádhu witnessed these horrors from a corner of the room and inwardly besought Allah to save him from the clutches of those demons. But Srikrishna, who was the bailiff of his circle, happened to see him and asked whether he had brought his rent. Sádhu got up, salámed humbly, and replied, "Babuji, you know my present circumstances well". "Answer yes or no," thundered Srikrishna, "I have no time to listen to your excuses."

"Your servant is a very poor man," continued Sádhu, shaking from head to foot.

"Who is this person?" inquired Ramani Babu.

"This is Sádhu Sheikh, of Simulgachi," was the bailiff's reply, "the very same rascal who gave evidence against your honour in that faujdári (criminal) case."

"Is that so?" roared Ramani Babu. "And the son of a pig owes me rent?"

"Now, please, do not abuse me, Babuji," protested Sádhu, "only listen to my tale for one minute!"

"What, you dare to bandy words with me, *haramzádá* (bastard)?" shouted Ramani Babu, rising from his seat. "Doorkeeper, let him have fifty cuts, laid on hard!"

Swish, swish, swish, sounded the nimble cane, and made a grey pattern on Sádhu's naked flesh. His screams and prayers for mercy were mocked by the obsequious crowd, and at length he fell senseless on the floor.

"Look, he is shamming," observed Ramani Babu; "drag him outside and souse him with water until he comes to." The command was obeyed, and when Sádhu was able to sit up he was brought back to the dreaded presence. Again his arrears of rent were demanded, and once more he feebly protested that he could not discharge them. Thereon Ramani Babu ordered him to be hung up. Forthwith, a dozen eager hands were laid on him, a rope was passed under his armpits, and the free end thrown over a rafter of the office. By this means he was hauled from the ground and swung suspended, a butt of sarcasm and abuse for Ramani Babu's myrmidons. After enduring this humiliation for an hour or so, he was let down and a final demand made on him for the arrears of rent. On his again asserting inability Ramani Babu ordered his hut to be levelled with the ground and pulse to be sown on its site, as a punishment for his disobedience. He was then allowed to leave the scene of his misery.

On reaching home he found Bemani seated in the porch, in expectation of his arrival. His fellow-victim said that he had lodged an information against Ramani Babu and his servants at the police station and intended going to Ghoria, next day, to complain to the Deputy Magistrate. Would Sádhu help him by giving evidence? he asked. "That I will," was the reply, "but I must first consult Jadunath Babu, who, I am sure, will help me." After Bemani's departure Sádhu went to his protector and told the story of his sufferings in full. Jadunath Babu bade him be of good cheer; for he would do all in his power to bring Ramani Babu to justice. Sádhu was comforted by this promise. He returned home and soon forgot all his sorrows in sleep.

About midnight he was aroused by voices in his yard, and, sallying forth, discovered a gang of clubmen employed by Ramani Babu, in the act of tearing the roof from his hut. Remonstrance was met by jeering and threats of violence; so the luckless man stood helplessly under a neighbouring tamarind tree, while his house was reduced to a heap of bamboos and thatch. The material was taken away in carts, the site dug up, and pulse sown thereon. Thus not a trace of Sádhu's home was left. He passed the remaining hours of the night under the tree; and early next morning he called on Jadu Babu, to whom he unfolded the story of this latest outrage. His patron boiled over with indignation. He sent Sádhu to the police station, in order to lay an information against his persecutors, promising to give him a house and land to compensate his losses. In less than a fortnight, the injured man was installed in a new hut and in possession of enough land to support him comfortably. Then he settled down, with heartfelt prayers for Jadu Babu's long life and prosperity. He even sent for his wife and a young sister-in-law, who had been staying with her brother near Calcutta.

Meantime Bemani had taken out a summons for causing grievous hurt against Ramani Babu and his servants. When the case came on for hearing before a Deputy Magistrate at Ghoria, all the accused pleaded "not guilty". They could not deny the fact that he had been beaten within an inch of his life, but alleged provocation on his part, inasmuch as he had fomented a rebellion among the ryots. Jadu Babu was not idle. He provided the complainant with first-rate legal advice and paid all the expenses of adducing witnesses. Emboldened by his support, at least a dozen of Ramani Babu's ryots who were present while he was being thrashed, came forward to give evidence of the brutal treatment he had received and to deny the counter charge brought by the defendants. Thus the case ended in the conviction of Ramani Babu and three of his servants, who were sentenced to fines aggregating Rs. 200. Then the charges preferred by Sádhu were taken up by the Deputy Magistrate. As they were of a far graver character, the barrister brought from Calcutta by Ramani Babu obtained a week's adjournment in order to procure rebutting evidence.

At this time the Muharram festival was in full swing. Sádhu was too busy in getting up his case to take part in it; but he sent his wife to some relatives at Ghoria, while his young sister-in-law, who was suffering from fever, remained at home. He was aroused one night by loud screams coming from the hut occupied by this girl. On running out to see what was the matter, he fell into the arms of a stranger who was crossing his yard in a desperate hurry. A struggle ensued, but the intruder managed to escape, not before Sádhu had recognised him as a ryot of Ramani Babu, named Karim. On asking his sister-in-law what had happened, the poor girl told him with many sobs that a man had broken into the hut, and awakened her by seizing her throat, but had been scared away by her screams. As soon as day dawned, Sádhu ran to the house of Karim's uncle, in the hope of finding him there. The uncle, however, declared that Karim had been absent since the previous evening, and on learning the grave charge preferred by Sádhu, he begged with folded hands that the scandal might be stifled, at any cost, for the sake of both families. Sádhu would promise nothing, but for obvious reasons he laid no information against Karim.

Two days later he was engaged on his evening meal, when a Sub-Inspector appeared. After asking whether his name was Sádhu, the policeman slipped a pair of handcuffs on his wrists and turned a deaf ear to his bewildered request for information as to the charge preferred against him. Thus he was ignominiously taken to the station lock-up, followed by a crowd, whom he begged to inform Jadu Babu of his trouble. The latter was speedily fetched by a compassionate neighbour, and, after conversing with the police officer, he told Sádhu that he was actually charged with murder! Karim's uncle had informed the police that, his nephew having disappeared since the day of the alleged trespass, he suspected Sádhu of foul play. An inquiry followed which led to Sádhu's transfer to the district jail.

Jadu Babu was certain that his enemy had instigated the charge, and knew that he was quite capable of suppressing Karim in order to get Sádhu into trouble.

He was advised by friends whom he consulted not to poke his nose into so ugly an affair: but his sense of justice prevailed. He went to Ghaneshyám Babu, whom he told the whole story related by Sádhu. On learning that Ramani Babu was implicated, the pleader saw an opportunity of wreaking vengeance on the persecutor of his brother. Gladly did he undertake the prisoner's defence.

In due course the charge preferred by Sádhu against Ramani Babu was heard by a Deputy Magistrate. With Ghaneshyám Babu's aid, the complainant proved it up to the hilt, and all concerned were heavily fined. Soon afterwards Sádhu himself appeared before the Deputy Magistrate to answer a charge of murder. The circumstantial evidence against him was so strong that he was committed to the Sessions Court. When brought up for trial there, he astounded his backers by pleading guilty and offering to point out the spot where he had buried Karim's corpse. The case was forthwith adjourned for a local inquiry; and the European District Superintendent of Police took Sádhu to the place indicated, where he had the soil turned up in all directions without result. Sádhu admitted that he was mistaken and piloted the police to another spot, where they again failed to discover any trace of the missing man. On these facts being reported to the judge, he fixed the morrow for final hearing.

At 11 A.M. he took his seat on the bench in a Court packed with eager spectators, and was reading a charge to the jury, strongly adverse to the prisoner, when an uproar was heard outside. Proceedings were suspended while the judge sent an usher to ascertain the cause; but ere he returned, half a dozen men burst into the courtroom crying *Dohai!* (justice!). Jadu Babu, who was one of the intruders, signalled the others to be silent, and thus addressed the judge with folded hands:—

"Your Honour, the dead has come to life! Here is Karim, who was supposed to have been murdered!"

There was a tremendous sensation in Court. When it subsided the judge thrust aside his papers and asked for evidence as to Karim's identity, which was soon forthcoming on oath. Then he ordered him to be sworn, and recorded the following deposition:—

"Incarnation of Justice! I will make a full confession, whatever may happen to me. I was sent for about a month ago by my landlord Ramani Babu, who ordered me to insult some woman of Sádhu's household, in order that he might be excommunicated. In fear of my life I consented to do so, and that very night I broke into the hut where Sádhu's sister-in-law lay asleep. Her cries attracted Sádhu, who grappled with me in his yard. However, I managed to escape, and on reporting my failure to Ramani Babu, he sent me in charge of a *Barkandáz* (guard) to Paliti, which is ten coss (20 miles) away. There I was confined in a *Kacheri* (office building) until yesterday, when I got away after nightfall. I had to pass through Ghoria Bazar, on my way home this morning, and there I ran up against Jadu Babu, who stopped and questioned me closely about my movements. There was nothing for me but to make a clean breast of everything. He took me to a babu's house where he was staying, and thence brought me to your honour's presence."

Karim's confession took every one by surprise, and it was corroborated by

Jadu Babu in the witness-box. The judge then asked Sadhu why he pleaded guilty.

"Incarnation of Justice," was the reply, "it was the Daroga Babu (Sub-Inspector of Police) who frightened me into making a confession. He told me again and again that he had quite enough evidence to hang me, and advised me to escape death by admitting the charge of murdering Karim. While I was shut up alone in jail, I had no one to consult or rely on. Through fear, my wits entirely left me and I resolved to obtain mercy by making a false confession."

These circumstances, strange as they may appear to the Western reader, were no novelty to the Sessions Judge. In charging the jury, he commented severely on the conduct of the station police and directed them to return a verdict of not guilty, which they promptly did.

Ghaneshyám Babu did not let the matter drop. He moved the District Magistrate to prosecute Ramani Babu and his bailiff, Srikrishna, for conspiring to charge an innocent man with murder. Both were brought to trial and, despite the advocacy of a Calcutta barrister, they each received a sentence of six months' rigorous imprisonment. Justice, lame-footed as she is, at length overtook a pair of notorious evil-doers.

THE BITER BITTEN.

Babu Chandra Mohan Bai, or Chandra Babu, as he was usually called, was a rich banker with many obsequious customers. He was a short choleric man, very fond of his hookah, without which he was rarely seen in public. He had no family, except a wife who served him uncomplainingly, and never received a letter or was known to write one except in the course of business. His birthplace, nay his caste, were mysteries. But wealth conceals every defect, and no one troubled to inquire into Chandra Babu's antecedents. This much was known—that he had come to Kadampur fifteen years before my tale opens with a brass drinking-pot and blanket, and obtained a humbly-paid office as a clerk under a local Zemindar. In this capacity he made such good use of the means it offered of extorting money that he was able to set up as a moneylender at Simulgachi, close to Kadampur. When people learnt that a new Shylock was at their service, they flocked to him in times of stress. His usual rate of interest being only 5 per cent, per mensem, he cut into the business of other moneylenders, and in four or five years had no serious competitor within a radius of four miles from Kadampur itself. Once master of the situation he drew in his horns, lending money only to people who could give ample security in land, government papers, or jewellery. He also started a *tejárati* business (loans of rice, for seed and maintenance during the "slack" months, repaid in kind, with heavy interest, after the harvest). Although few *Khátaks* (customers) were able to extricate their property from his clutches or clear off their debit balances, Chandra Babu continued to be in great request. He was heard to boast that every family in or near Kadampur, except the Basus, were on his books. The rapid growth of his dealings compelled him to engage a *gomastha* (manager) in the person of Santi Priya Dás, who had been a village schoolmaster notorious for cruelty. The duties of his new office were entirely to Santi Priya's liking, and he performed them to Chandra Babu's unqualified approval.

On a certain morning in late August, Chandra Babu sat in his office to receive applications for money or grain. One of his customers named Karim Sheikh came in and squatted close to the door, after salaming profoundly. On seeing him Chandra Babu at once remembered that his bond had run out on 15th July, and that he owed nearly Rs. 100, principal and interest. He therefore addressed the newcomer in accents of wrath. "What do you want here, you son of a pig?"

"Babuji," pleaded Karim, "my stars are unlucky. You know how wretched the rice harvest has been."

"Yes, we know all that," replied Santi, who sat near his master. "It's the old story, when people who can pay won't pay. Have you brought the money, eh?"

Karim was obliged to confess he had not.

"Then why have you come here?" roared Chandra Babu. "To show your face, I suppose. We see hundreds of better-looking fellows than you daily. You have got to pay up at once, you *badmásh* (rascal)."

Karim's wrath was stirred by this expression. He replied, "Now, Babu, don't be abusive; I won't stand it".

"What, do you want to teach me manners, Maulvie Saheb (doctor learned in Mohammadan law)?" asked Chandra Babu sarcastically.

An exchange of compliments followed which were not altogether to Shylock's advantage, and at length he roared, "Get out of this office, you rascal, and look out for squalls! I'll sell you up!" Karim left in high dudgeon, inviting Chandra Babu to do his worst, and the latter forthwith concocted a scheme of vengeance with his manager.

Next day Santi obtained a summons against Karim from the Munsiff (civil judge of first instance) of Ghoria and, by bribing the court process-server, induced him to make a false return of service. In due course the suit came on for hearing, and as the defendant was of course absent, it was decreed against him *ex parte*. Execution being also granted, Santi accompanied the court bailiff to Karim's house, where they seized all his movable property and carried it off to the Court, leaving him in bewilderment and tears. He was unable to tear himself away from his gutted home but sat for hours under a tree hard by, pondering on his ill-fortune. Not until the sun had set and village cattle began to file in from pasture, did he cast one lingering look on the scene of his childhood and walk away with a sigh, whither no one cared to inquire.

A week later, however, Karim strode into Chandra Babu's office attended by two friends, and counted out ten ten-rupee notes, which he handed to the moneylender, with a peremptory request to release his chattels at once. Chandra Babu was greatly surprised by the turn matters had taken, but he was not the man to let property slip from his clutches. So he asked Santi whether the debtor did not owe a bill of costs. The manager referred to his books and declared that Rs. 33 8. 0. were still due. Karim planked down the money without further ado and asked for a receipt, which Santi reluctantly gave him. Then he again demanded the immediate release of his property. On receiving an evasive answer, he remarked that Chandra Babu would hear from him shortly and left the office.

About a month later, Chandra Babu was aroused from sleep in the dead of night by shouts coming from his inner courtyard. He jumped up and popped his head out of the window, but withdrew it hastily on seeing twenty or thirty men running about his premises, with lighted torches, and shouting—"Loot! loot!" Paralysed by fear, he crawled under the bed and lay in breathless expectation of further developments. Presently the door was forced open, and a crowd poured into the room. Chandra Babu's hiding place was soon discovered by the dacoits (gang robbers), who dragged him out by the legs and demanded his keys on pain of instant death. Seeing a rusty *talwár* (sword) flourished within an inch of his throat, the unhappy man at once produced them, whereon the dacoits opened his safe and took out several bags of rupees. Then at a signal from their *sardar* (leader), they bound Chandra Babu hand and foot and squatted round him in a circle. The sardar thus addressed him:—

"Babuji, do you know us?"

"How can I know you?" groaned their victim. "Your faces are blackened and concealed by your turbans. Gentlemen, I implore you to spare my life! I never injured any of you."

"Indeed!" replied the sardar sarcastically; "you have been the ruin of us all. Look you, Chandra Babu, we are all *Khátaks* (customers) of yours whom you have fleeced by levying exorbitant interest on loans and falsifying our accounts. It's no use going to law for our rights; you are hand in glove with the civil court *amla* (clerks) and *peons* (menials) and can get them to do whatever you wish. So we have determined to take the law into our own hands. We have made up our accounts and find that you have extorted from us Rs. 5,000, over and above advances of rice and cash with reasonable interest. Now we're going to help ourselves to that sum, besides damages at four annas in the rupee (twenty-five per cent.). This makes just Rs. 6,250 you owe us."

Thereon the dacoits counted out cash to that amount and no more, which was placed in bags containing Rs. 1,000 each, ready for removal. Chandra Babu heaved a sigh of relief, thinking that he had got off rather cheaply, but his troubles were not at an end. The sardar came close to him and asked:—

"Look at me carefully: do you know me?"

"No bábá, but you are my son. Pray, spare my life! See, I am half dead already and ruined as well!"

"I am Karim Sheikh," said the sardar impressively.

"So you are," replied Chandra Babu, after recovering from his intense surprise; "but why have you turned dacoit?"

"It was owing to your oppression, which drove me from my house, and deprived me of the means of livelihood. All my companions here have been beggared by you, and scores of other families too. The whole of Kadampur and Simulgachi are clamouring for your blood, and Allah has appointed me to be the minister of his vengeance. Time was when I had to cringe to you, just as you are doing to me, but never did I receive mercy from you. Now the tables are turned. I might kill you, and who would dare to inform the police folk?" (Here Karim made a vicious prod with his talwár, which passed within half an inch of the terror-stricken victim's throat.) "I might put you out of caste by slaying one of your cows and forcing you to eat its flesh. You deserve all this and more—but we will be merciful. Swear by your goddesses Kali and Durga that you will never in future demand more than four annas in the rupee yearly for loans of money or rice. Swear that you will never again bribe the amla or peons of the Courts; swear that you will never again falsify the accounts of your Khátaks."

Chandra Babu took the oaths demanded with an appearance of unction and then implored his captors to release him.

"Wait a minute," was Karim's reply, "we must collect our belongings."

So saying he ordered the dacoits to extinguish their torches and follow him with the bags of money. He led them to a ravine on the river bank, about a *coss* (two miles) distant, where the spoil was equitably divided according to a list of names and amounts due in Karim's possession. Then after arranging for alibis in case of criminal proceedings, the band dispersed, well satisfied with their night's work.

Chandra Babu's neighbours made no sign until the dacoits were well out of hearing, when they flocked in to unloose his bonds and offer hypocritical condolences. The village Chaukidar (watchman) was sent off to the police station, and next day arrived the Sub-Inspector with a posse of constables to investigate the dacoity. After recording the complainant's statement, they endeavoured to secure additional evidence, but Chandra Babu was so cordially disliked, and the dacoits' vengeance so dreaded, that not a soul came forward to corroborate his story. Karim was arrested, with half a dozen accomplices named by Chandra Babu. They had no difficulty in proving that they were attending a wedding ceremony five miles away on the night of the alleged dacoity. So the case was reported to headquarters as false; and Chandra Babu escaped prosecution for deceiving the police, by giving a heavy bribe to the Sub-Inspector.

His evil star continued in the ascendant. About a week afterwards, he discovered a heavy deficit in his cash book, kept by Santi Priya, which that rascal failed to explain, and next day the trusty manager did not attend office. Indeed he has never been heard of since. This new calamity was Chandra Babu's "last straw". He hastened to realise outstanding debts and left the village, bag and baggage, to the intense relief of its inhabitants, who celebrated his exit by offering *pujá* or *namáz* (Mohammadan prayers) according to the religion they severally professed.

ALL'S WELL THAT END'S WELL.

Every good Hindu feels bound to get his daughter or sister, as the case may be, married before she attains puberty. Rich people find little difficulty in securing suitable matches for their girls; but Babu Jadunath Basu, widely known as "Jadu Babu," was not blessed with a large share of this world's goods; and his sister Basumati was close on her teens. The marriage-broker had certainly suggested more than one aspirant for her hand, but they were not to Jadu Babu's liking. As years rolled by, his anxiety deepened into despair. A match was at length offered which was passably good, although it did not answer Jadu Babu's expectations. He learnt from private inquiry that the boy proposed bore a good character, never mixed with doubtful associates, and had no constitutional defect. Hindu parents are very careful to ascertain the health of a suitor, and should they suspect any inherited disease, such as consumption, they reject him remorselessly. It must not be supposed that such lads are always doomed to celibacy, for their unsoundness may be hidden or counterbalanced by a substantial money payment.

Jadu Babu found out that the boy had matriculated at Calcutta and was attending the second year class at a Metropolitan College; more important still, his father, Amarendra Babu, had money invested in Government paper, besides a substantial brick house—qualifications which augured well for his sister's wedded happiness. The next step was to invite his own father, Kumodini Babu, to come from Benares and help him to clinch matters. The old man pleaded that he had done with the world and all its vanities; so Jadu Babu had to make a pilgrimage to the Holy City, where he induced Kumodini Babu to return home with him. Three days later the pair went to Calcutta with two friends, in order to make the suitor's acquaintance. They were welcomed by Amarendra Babu, who at once sent for his son. The boy came in with eyes fixed on the ground and shyly took a seat near Kumodini Babu. He underwent a severe scrutiny, and at last the old man broke silence by asking the lad his name. Being informed that it was Samarendra Nath, he inquired the names of his father and grandfather, which were promptly given.

"Good boy," observed Kumodini Babu, "the times are so completely out of joint that youths are ashamed to utter their father's name, let alone their grandfather's. Where are you studying?"

"At the Metropolitan Institution," was the reply.

"An excellent college," said Kumodini Babu; then after a whispered consultation with Jadu Babu, he said, "I am delighted with Samarendra's modesty and good manners, and have no objection whatever to giving my daughter to him in marriage—provided *Prajapati* (the Lord of All) causes no hitch". Samarendra thought that his ordeal was over, but he was mistaken. One of Kumodini Babu's friends, who happened to be a Calcutta B.A., would not lose the opportunity of airing his superior learning.

"What are your English text-books?" he asked.

"Blackie's *Self-culture,* Helps' *Essays,* Milton's *Paradise Lost,* and Tennyson's *Enoch Arden,*" gabbled Samarendra in one breath.

"Very good, now please fetch your *Paradise Lost.*"

The boy disappeared, returning shortly with a well-thumbed volume, which the B.A. opened and selected Satan's famous apostrophe to the Sun for explanation. Samarendra was speechless. After waiting for a minute, the B.A. asked what text-book he studied in physics and was told that it was Ganot's *Natural Philosophy.* He asked Samarendra to describe an electrophone, whereon the lad began to tremble violently. Kumodini Babu had pity on his confusion and told him to run away. Needless to say he was promptly obeyed.

It has become a Calcutta custom for possible fathers-in-law to cross-examine suitors on their text-books; but few boys are able to satisfy the test, however brilliant their acquirements may be. Poor Samarendra was too overwhelmed with the strangeness of his position to do himself justice.

When the elder folks were quite alone they plunged into business. Kumodini Babu sounded his host as to *dena paona* (settlements) on either side; but the latter courteously left them entirely to his discretion. It was settled that Basumati's *pákká dekhá* (betrothal) should be celebrated on 12th November at Kumodini Babu's, and that of Samarendra's at his father's, two days later.

Basumati being an only daughter, Kumodini Babu determined to conduct her marriage on a magnificent scale. In anticipation of the betrothal feast, he brought three Brahman cooks from Calcutta to prepare curries, *pillaos* and sweetmeats under the supervision of the ladies of his household.

At length the auspicious day came round. At 5 P.M. Amarendra Babu, with half a dozen friends, arrived at Kumodini Babu's house from Calcutta. They were received with great courtesy and conducted to seats, where a plentiful supply of tobacco and betel awaited them. At half-past seven, Jadu Babu presented the bride-elect to her future family. She looked charming in a Parsi shawl and Victoria jacket, decked out with glittering jewels, and sat down near Amarendra Babu, after saluting him respectfully. He took up some *dhán, durba* and *chandan* (paddy, bent grass and sandal-wood paste) and blessed her, presenting her at the same time with a gold *chur* (bracelet). After again saluting him, the timid girl was led back to the inner apartments. Then the guests were taken to a large hall where supper was ready for their delectation. Full justice was done to the repast; and after it was over, they washed their hands in the yard and smoked or chewed betel in perfect bliss until half-past ten. Then Amarendra Babu asked leave to return by the last train, declining hospitality for the night on the plea of previous engagements. While saying "good-bye" he called Jadu Babu aside and thrust Rs. 30 into his hands, to be distributed among the *guru* (spiritual guide), *purohit* (family priest), and servants.

Two days afterwards, Kumodini Babu and his son went to Calcutta for the boy's betrothal. He blessed Samarendra, presenting him with a gold mohur (an obsolete coin worth sixteen rupees) besides Rs. 50 for the priest and servants of his household. A feast followed on the same scale as the previous one.

Kumodini Babu's family priest decided that Ásár 28th would be a lucky day for the wedding, which was to be held at the bride's great-uncle's house in Calcutta. Early on the 26th, the Gaihálud (turmeric smearing) ceremony took place. Amarendra Babu rubbed his son's body with a mixture of turmeric and oil and despatched a supply to Kumodini Babu by his own barber, with injunctions to have it applied to his daughter's person before 9 A.M., because subsequent hours would be inauspicious. On the barber's arrival, the ladies of Kumodini Babu's household anointed Basumati with turmeric and oil and clad her in a gorgeous wrapper. Then they conducted her to another room where a *jánti* (instrument for cracking betel-nuts) was given her and certain *nitkits* (minor ceremonies) were performed.

At 11 A.M. the presents given on the occasion of the turmeric-smearing (gaihálud) were brought by twenty servants who were regaled with a feast made ready in anticipation of their arrival. After partaking of it they were dismissed with a largesse of one rupee each. During the next two days presents continued to pour in from relatives of both families.

At length the fateful 28th Ásár dawned, bringing a mighty commotion in the respective houses. Shouts and laughter echoed from every side. Amarendra Babu had resolved to marry his son in a style which, sooth to say, was far above his means, hoping to recoup himself from the large cash payment which he expected from Kumodini Babu. On his side the latter had consulted relatives as to the proper dowry. All agreed that Rs. 2,000 worth of ornaments; Rs. 1,001 in cash; Rs. 500 for *Barabharan* (gifts to a bridegroom); and Rs. 500 for *Phúlsajya* (lit. a bed of flowers) would be sufficient. Thus Kumodini Babu provided Rs. 4,001 and imagined that he was acting generously.

At 7.30 P.M. the bridegroom's procession was formed. A Sub-Inspector of Police and three constables led the way, followed by a band of music. Next came a carriage and four conveying Samarendra, his younger brother, and the family priest. Carriages belonging to Amarendra Babu's friends, and some hired ones full of invited guests, brought up the rear. When a start was made, the little police force hustled vehicles out of the way and even stopped tram-cars when necessary; while the band tortured selections from Handel and Beethoven to the intense delight of passers-by, many of whom paused to criticise shortcomings in the procession among themselves. In about an hour it reached its destination, where Kumodini Babu's uncle received the guests. The family barber carried Samarendra in his arms to a chair which had been provided for him. There he sat with eyes fixed steadily on the ground, while his friends squatted round and cracked jokes at his expense. He smiled, but modestly implored them not to put him out of countenance. The *Lagna* (auspicious time) was determined to be 9.30; meanwhile the guests sat on carpets or chairs, beguiling the delay with hookahs.

While mirth was at its height, strange things were happening in a private room adjoining. Soon after arriving, Amarendra Babu asked Kumodini Babu and Jadunath to display the presents destined for the young couple. They took him into a room where all were set forth to the best advantage. After examining them in silence awhile, Amarendra Babu kicked the nearest contemptuously aside, remarking that they were "mere rubbish". In point of fact he fully expected Kumodini Babu to give Rs. 4,000 in cash, Rs. 2,000 in respect of Barabharan and Phulsajya and Rs. 4,000 worth of jewellery—Rs. 10,000 in all. To judge by the ornaments shown him, the total dowry would be barely half as much and he could not help expressing disappointment. On asking Kumodini Babu what he intended paying down in cash, and learning that Rs. 1,001 was all he could afford, Amarendra Babu's indignation knew no bounds. He demanded Rs. 5,000, declaring that if it were not paid on the nail, he would take his son away! The wretched father implored twelve hours' delay, but was told in as many words that his promise could not be relied on. The deadlock soon got wind, and Amarendra Babu's action was severely commented on by the guests, but he remained obdurate. Kumodini Babu's uncle ran to a wealthy acquaintance for a loan of Rs. 4,000, but was told that so large a sum was not available at short notice. On his return, Amarendra Babu delivered his ultimatum—Rs. 4,000 cash to be paid forthwith; and finding that it was hopeless to expect so much, he hailed a cab, hurried Samarendra into it, and drove home in high dudgeon, followed by all his relatives and friends. This unexpected calamity brought mourning into a house of mirth; people spoke in whispers; and anguish left its mark on every face.

Shám Babu was supervising the Hálûikars (confectioners) when the awful news reached his ears. For a few minutes he stood transfixed to the spot; but ere long a happy thought struck him. He clapped his hands in silent glee, and ran to an inner room, where Kumodini Babu lay groaning on the bare floor, guarded by his son who feared that he would do something rash.

"Mahásay," he said soothingly. "Do not take on like this! God's ways are inscrutable; perchance He has broken the match off for your daughter's good."

"Yes, God's will be done," replied Kumodini Babu in sepulchral tones. "We are but His instruments." Then after a pause he added, "What I dread most is loss of caste".

"Who will dare to excommunicate you for such a trifle?" asked Shám Babu indignantly.

"Alas, you know too well that my family's position in society is terribly compromised. A marriage postponed is a marriage lost!" groaned Kumodini Babu.

"But why should it be postponed?" was Sham Babu's eager question. "I have a proposal to make, if you will only give it a moment's thought."

Kumodini Babu looked up, and a ray of hope dried his tears; he waited anxiously for further particulars.

"You know my son Susil, I suppose? He is just sixteen and has passed the Entrance Examination."

"Yes, yes," answered Kumodini Babu. "He is a fine lad, obedient and well-mannered. But what has he got to do with our present fix?"

"Will you give your daughter to him in marriage? I will not ask a single pice as dowry."

Kumodini Babu sprang to his feet and embraced Shám Babu with fervour, saying, "You have saved my life. Personally, I should be delighted to have Susil as a son-in-law, but you must let me consult my son and wife." He ran to the inner apartments, and communicated Shám Babu's offer to his near relatives. This unexpected solution of the dilemma filled them with surprise; and a loud clamour of voices echoed through the house. Finally all, without exception, agreed that the match would be an excellent one. Kumodini Babu brought news of its acceptance to Shám Babu, and it spread among the wedding guests, who were loud in their praises of his true Hindu spirit.

Shám Babu went into the courtyard where Susil sat talking with some other boys about the astounding piece of good fortune which awaited him. That he, the son of a humble clerk, should espouse the daughter of a Zemindar was more than his wildest dreams had anticipated. He joyfully accompanied Shám Babu to a room, where he was clad in silken attire, and thence to the hall, where he was solemnly inducted into the empty bridegroom's chair amid the acclamations of the assembled guests. As the *Lagna* (auspicious time) had not run out the actual marriage ceremony began forthwith. Basumati was given away by her father; while the ladies performed *Satpák* (lit. going round seven times—a ceremony without which a Hindu marriage is not binding) and other minor ceremonies with zest. After all had been well and duly gone through, the bride and bridegroom were conducted to an inner apartment. Susil underwent the customary "chaff" from the ladies, which he bore with great good humour and was at last left alone with his young companion for life; while some of the fair guests sang wedding songs to the intense delight of their friends. Nor were the men-folk idle. They sat down to a sumptuous feast prepared for the recreant bridegroom's family, nor did they separate till daybreak.

At 3 P.M. on the morrow Shám Babu took Susil and Basumati to his own home, where the *Bau-Bhát* ceremony was performed in grand style. It was attended by all their caste-fellows, who were loud in extolling his magnanimity. Shám Babu accepted their praises meekly, remarking that he had done nothing more than his duty, by neglecting which he would have rendered himself accountable to God.

AN OUTRAGEOUS SWINDLE.

Amarendra Babu had expected Kumodini Babu to run after him, with entreaties to return and the promise of a note of hand for Rs. 4,000. Disappointment became downright wrath when he heard that his son's prospective bride had been forthwith married to another boy. After pondering awhile on this grievance, he sent an anonymous letter to Shám Babu's employers, to the effect that their clerk was robbing them right and left and running a business of his own with their money, under a fictitious name. They had implicit confidence in his honesty, and the only action they took was to hand the scrawl to him with a remark that they hoped he would discover and prosecute the writer.

Meanwhile Amarendra Babu cast about him for a suitable match for his son. Hearing of a likely girl from the marriage-broker, he visited her parents, who accepted his overtures with alacrity. The young lady's father, Jogesh by name, was a commission agent, whose regular earnings did not exceed thirty rupees a month; but he lived in such style that his neighbours believed him to be comfortably off. Amarendra Babu, too, was deceived by appearances, while the girl, who was exhibited to him, seemed intelligent and pretty. On his side, Jogesh knew his visitor to be a house-owner of some means; and learning from him that his son was a second-year student, he gladly consented to the match. The pair next broached a delicate question, that of dowry. Amarendra Babu had learnt by bitter experience of the folly of pitching expectations too high. He told Jogesh that he should be quite satisfied with Rs. 4,001, *viz.*, ornaments 2,000, *barabharan* and *phulsajya* Rs. 500 each, and cash Rs. 1,001. On Jogesh's expressing willingness to provide that amount, the *purohit* (family priest) was sent for who, after referring to a *panjika* (almanac), announced that Srában 20th would be an auspicious day for the marriage. They then separated with many protestations of mutual good-will.

Meantime Jogesh made minute inquiries as to Amarendra Babu's position and the health of his son. Their result was satisfactory enough; not so the fiasco related in my last chapter, which reached him with amplification, and made him resolve that Amarendra Babu should not play such tricks on him. He ordered no ornaments for his daughter, because he had little cash or credit, but simply borrowed Rs. 300 to meet absolutely necessary expenses. On the afternoon of Srában 20th he called in half a dozen city roughs, armed them with thick sticks, and plied them with spirits, telling them on no account to appear in the public apartments of his house until they received a signal agreed on.

At seven o'clock Amarendra Babu, with his son and an uncle named Rashbehari, arrived at Jogesh's house in a second-class cab. No procession attended them, partly because the last had cost so much money, partly owing to the fear that another hitch might cover them with ridicule. After exchanging hearty salutations with Jogesh, they asked him to exhibit the ornaments prepared for the bride-elect. He took them to a side room and left them there a while, presently introducing a well-dressed man as his family goldsmith. The latter unlocked a tin box which he was carrying and took out a number of glittering gold trinkets, one by one. After examining them carefully, Amarendra Babu asked him to weigh them, which he did, proving that their weight exceeded 120 *bháris* (forty-eight ounces), and their total value, at Rs. 20 per *bhári*, no less than Rs. 2,400. This was far more than he had bargained for, and Amarendra Babu was highly delighted; but his uncle insisted on sending for his own goldsmith to weigh the ornaments. Jogesh at once fell in with the suggestion, and this tradesman, on arrival, valued them at Rs. 2,700.

Rashbehari Babu's scepticism vanished, and he assented to his nephew's whispered hint that they need not ask Jogesh to produce the *barabharan*. He, however, insisted on satisfying them as to its worth and placed in their hands a heavy gold watch by McCabe, with an albert chain, equally ponderous; and assured them that he had paid Rs. 800 for the two. Amarendra's joy was perhaps excessive, and when the *lagna* (auspicious time) came round, he permitted the marriage to be celebrated. Every ceremony went off without a hitch, and the evening closed in feasting and mirth.

On the following afternoon Amarendra Babu took the bridegroom and bride with the box of ornaments to his own home, while Rashbehari Babu remained behind at Jogesh's to receive the cash. On mentioning this little formality he was assured that the sum of Rs. 1,001 had been duly counted out to his nephew; so he took his leave. When he reached home, he discovered the dirty trick that had been played by Jogesh. Amarendra stoutly denied having received any cash; and the tin box was proved to contain only fragments of brick neatly wrapped in paper, and covered with pink cotton wool.

The pair of dupes hurried to Jogesh's house for an explanation. He sat in the parlour, in evident expectation of their arrival, and asked with an air of unconcern what was the matter.

"You son of a pig!" roared Amarendra Babu, shaking his clenched fist close to Jogesh's nose. "Tell me where are the ornaments—where is the cash?"

"Why, did you not take away a box full of trinkets? and you must admit that the Rs. 1,001 were handed you in a cotton bag,"

This impudence was too much. Both uncle and nephew fell upon Jogesh and belaboured him sorely with their shoes. He did not retaliate, but consoled himself with the thought that he had done his duty, to God and society, by marrying his daughter, whatever fate might await him. After vowing to bring a suit against the swindler, Amarendra Babu and his uncle left the premises and did what they would have done much earlier had they not been in such a desperate hurry to marry the lad. They made inquiries as to Jogesh's position and soon discovered that he was a man of straw, quite unworthy of powder and shot. They learned, too, that he had hired Rs. 3,000 worth of trinkets for one night from a goldsmith, who never let them out of his possession. From a wealthy neighbour he had borrowed a McCabe's watch and chain, also for one night only. His arrangements made with a gang of city roughs, in order to prevent the marriage being broken off, also came to light. Amarendra Babu saw that he had been dealing with a cunning and desperate man and prudently determined to give him a wide berth in future. But his daughter was in Amarendra Babu's clutches, and she was forced to expiate the sins of her father. The luckless girl was kept on very short commons and locked into a dark room when she was not engaged in rough household work. Contrary to custom, she was not sent to her father's house three days after the marriage; nor was the *Bau-Bhát* ceremony performed. But Jogesh was on the alert; he managed to communicate with her by bribing a maid-servant, and one morning Amarendra Babu's household discovered that the half-starved bird had flown.

A year passed away without news of the truants; but, one evening, Amarendra Babu was sitting in his parlour, spelling out a spicy leader in the *Indian Mirror*, when, to his unqualified amazement, Jogesh stepped in and unbidden took a seat. Amarendra Babu's first impulse was to shout for help and eject the intruder with every species of ignominy, but second thoughts are proverbially peaceful.

"This Jogesh," he reflected, "must be a very smart fellow, or he would never have taken us all in as he did. It is better to be on the side of the sacrificial knife than the goat that awaits its stroke. Why should I not hear what he has to say? He would not have come here without some excellent reason—perhaps he wants to pay up part of his debt to me, or maybe he has some scheme with money in it to unfold. He'll certainly try to overreach me again; but then once bitten twice shy. I'll be on my guard." Then with an attempt at irony he asked:—

"What brings you of all people to my house? Have you got another daughter to marry?"

Had Amarendra Babu observed the gleam which shot from Jogesh's shifty eyes, he would have kicked him out at once, but he waited for a reply, which came in honeyed accents:—

"Now, Babuji, please don't rake up old stories; what is done cannot be undone. You, as a father, ought to excuse little subterfuges, contrived in order to get a daughter off one's hands. I was so anxious to ally myself with your distinguished family that I *did* sail rather near the wind. But I have come to offer you some amends by putting you on a really good thing."

Amarendra Babu's cupidity was excited by these words. He asked with apparent indifference: "Well, let me hear more of your famous plans, and meantime I'll call for a hookah".

Jogesh was overjoyed by the success of his manoeuvres. He answered, punctuating his sentences by inhaling fragrant *Bhilsi*, "You have heard of Campbell & Co., the big cooly recruiters of Azimganj? Well, they have an agency in Calcutta for supplying emigrants to Mauritius, Trinidad, and other outlandish places; and it is run by one Ganesh Sen who is a close friend of mine. He tells me that a number of sub-contracts will be given out to-morrow, and I have made up my mind to apply for one. Ganesh Babu is sure to come to terms with me; and I know a very smart *sardár* (ganger) who will supply me with any number of coolies I want. But I shall take care to keep a large margin between the rate per head, at which they will be delivered to Campbell & Co., and that which my sardár will receive. All this will be clear profit."

"It seems a good speculation," said Amarendra Babu musingly, "but I should like to have further particulars. What do you expect to make per head delivered; and what capital will be required?" Jogesh pulled out a paper covered with calculations, and proved to his host's satisfaction that as much as Rs. 5 might be expected on each cooly. As for capital, a few hundreds would be needed in the first instance as an advance to the sardár, and other sums later, to provide outfits for the coolies according to law. Campbell & Co. settled the accounts of sub-contractors monthly, so that Amarendra would not have to wait long for his money. Jogesh concluded by urging his *baibáhik* (father of a son-in-law) to call with him on Messrs. Campbell & Co.'s Calcutta manager, who would corroborate his statements. Amarendra Babu thought that there would be no harm in going into matters further. He fixed 4 P.M. on the following day for a visit to 809 Strand, where Campbell & Co.'s branch offices were said to be located.

On arriving there punctually, he was met by Jogesh, who took him through a courtyard where twenty or thirty coolies were squatting, shepherded by a stalwart Mohammadan, wearing a blue turban, who was introduced as Salim Sardár, his ganger. Pushing through the little crowd, they entered a well-furnished office, where several clerks sat writing busily. One of them looked up when Jogesh said: "Ganesh Babu, I have brought you my *baibáhik*, who is thinking of joining me in a sub-contract".

The manager, for such he was, received Amarendra Babu politely and said that he would gladly come to terms with them. He then produced a written contract in duplicate on stamped paper, by which the partners agreed to furnish at least 1,000 coolies monthly, during the emigration season, at rates which left a net profit of Rs. 5 per head, to be shared equally between them. After reading both documents over twice, Amarendra Babu executed them, as did Jogesh; and the former took possession of his copy. On returning home with his new partner, he entered on a discussion as to ways and means. It was agreed that he should advance Rs. 5,000 for preliminaries, which he did a week later, raising the amount on a mortgage of his Calcutta house property. Everything went swimmingly at first; Jogesh calling daily to report progress; and a month later he burst into Amarendra Babu's parlour, with a cash-book and bundle of currency notes. The latter learnt to his intense delight that his share of the profits amounted to Rs. 1268 12.4. which was promptly paid him. Two or three days afterwards Jogesh again called to tell him that an opportunity of making Rs. 10,000 net had occurred owing to the pressing demand for cooly freight from a ship which was lying half-empty, and costing large sums for demurrage. Rs. 10,000 must be forthcoming at once for advances and perhaps special railway trucks, but Amarendra Babu might calculate on receiving 100 per cent. in three weeks at the latest. Such a chance of money-making was not to be lost. Amarendra Babu rushed off to his broker and sold nearly all his Government paper for Rs. 10,000 in cash, which he handed to Jogesh, against a formal acknowledgment.

Seeing nothing of his partner for several days, Amarendra called to inquire how the new contract fared and was thunderstruck to find Jogesh's house locked up. Hastening to Campbell & Co.'s Strand offices, he saw a notice "to let" exhibited there. This spectacle confirmed his worst fears—he had been twice swindled outrageously. His only hope lay in the scoundrel's arrest; so he laid an information at the police station, and a clever detective was told off to investigate the charge. Strange was the story which came to light. No such firm as "Campbell & Co." existed; Ganesh Babu and Salim Sardár were both accomplices of Jogesh, who had rented an office on the Strand for one month at Rs. 300 which was never paid. He had also engaged twenty or thirty loafers at 4 annas (4d.) a head to personate coolies for a couple of hours. This part of the inquiry was satisfactory enough—for the police; not so the efforts they made to trace Jogesh and his accomplices. From that day to this nothing has been heard of them.

Amarendra Babu never recovered from this crushing blow. The loss of nearly Rs. 14,000 is a very serious matter for any one of moderate means; to him it was doubly grievous, for he worshipped money and valued nothing but success. By constantly brooding on his misfortunes and folly he developed symptoms of madness and was at times so violent that his relatives were obliged to confine him in a dark room. One afternoon he eluded their vigilance and hurried to the office of "Campbell & Co." on the Strand. After gazing for several minutes at the empty building, he heaved a deep sigh, ran across the road, and sprang into the River Hughli. The undercurrent sucked his body in, and it was never recovered. Perhaps Mother Ganges was loath to keep a carcase so tainted in her bosom, and so whirled it southwards to the ocean.

THE VIRTUE OF ECONOMY.

Shám Babu was a clerk of nearly thirty years' standing, and the approach of old age made him anxious to escape from the daily grind of business. He asked permission to resign, which was reluctantly granted; his employers signifying their appreciation of his faithful service by granting him a pension of Rs. 30 a month and offering to provide for any of his relatives who might be fit for clerical work. Shám Babu thanked them warmly and retired to his native village, with the intention of passing the evening of life in peace. He had always lived well within his means. People who were thrice as rich could not imagine how he contrived to bring up a family on the salary which he was known to enjoy. Some folks insinuated that he had made money by giving his son in marriage to Kumodini Babu's daughter, never remembering that a dowry is reserved for the bride's benefit, while the cash payment made to a father-in-law barely suffices to meet the expenses of elaborate nuptial ceremonies. Others hinted that he had waxed rich on illicit commissions—another charge which was quite without foundation. Shám Babu was strictly honest, and besides, the opportunities within the reach of clerks employed by a private firm are not worth mentioning.

After settling down at Kadampur he cudgelled his brains for some means of increasing his slender resources. Friends advised him to try farming, or start a business in lending grain to cultivators. Neither trade was to his liking. Clerks are of little use outside their own sphere; and Shám Babu was too soft-hearted to succeed as a village Shylock. A matter of pressing importance was to establish his son Susil, who had passed the First Arts examination and was hanging about the Government offices at Ghoria, in the hope of securing a post. Shám Babu took advantage of his late employer's offer and sent the young man off to Calcutta armed with a sheaf of certificates. To his great delight, Susil was appointed clerk on Rs. 25—a magnificent start, which relieved his father's most pressing anxiety.

Shám Babu had begun life with a small patrimony which was slowly increased by savings from his monthly pay. He was worth nearly Rs. 10,000, the whole of which was lent by him to a trader named Gopál Datta, certified by Shám Babu's brother-in-law Hari to be thoroughly trustworthy. This Gopál dealt in jute; and being a man of great daring, he speculated so successfully with Shám Babu's money that, within three or four years, he amassed a fortune of two lakhs (£13,333). He paid 12 per cent. interest on the loan regularly, which made a comfortable addition to Shám Babu's pension.

It was the latter's habit to visit his Calcutta relatives at least once a month. So, one day in June, 18—, he went to Hari Babu's house with the intention of passing the night there. His brother-in-law was absent and not expected till the morrow; but Shám Babu was welcomed by the ladies of the family, who made all arrangements for his comfort. In the evening he sat in the Baitakhana (parlour) reading the *Bhagavat Gita* (a mystical poem). A carriage drove up to the door whence alighted Rámanáth Babu, who was Gopál's younger brother. After the usual compliments had been exchanged, Shám Babu asked what business his visitor was engaged in.

"I have started as a broker in jute and oil-seeds," was the reply.

"I hope you will do as well as Gopál," said Shám Babu, "but I suppose you have joined him?"

"Certainly not," replied Rámanáth impulsively; then he checked himself, as though he had said too much.

Shám Babu was astonished by the tone adopted by his visitor. He asked, "Why, what's the matter with Gopál, nothing wrong I hope and trust?"

"No, not exactly; but I'm in a hurry to-day, you must excuse my taking leave."

Shám Babu, however, would not be put off with vague insinuations. He said, "I must ask you, Rámanáth, to be more precise. You know your brother has borrowed Rs. 10,000 from me on a mere note of hand, and I am naturally very anxious to learn the truth."

Rámanáth Babu paused for a few seconds before replying. "It is a fact that my brother's speculations have been unfortunate of late. He certainly made a good deal of money at one time, but sunk the bulk of it in bricks and mortar, which you know are not easily turned into liquid capital. You, as a large creditor, ought to be told how the land lies."

"This is the first I have heard of Gopál's difficulties," groaned Shám Babu.

"Yes, because no one troubled himself to tell you the truth; but I can assure you that Gopál's liabilities are something awful, and it is quite possible that he may have to take insolvency proceedings."

"You don't say so! What shall I do? If Gopál becomes bankrupt, I shall be utterly ruined."

"Well, I cannot advise you fully," replied Rámanáth Babu, "but forewarned is forearmed. If I were in your shoes I would certainly call in my loan." Thereon he took leave.

Shám Babu passed a restless night, dreaming of the debtor's jail and a starving family. On Hari Babu's return, next morning, he related the purport of his conversation with Rámanáth. His host said: "You should not attach too much importance to such tittle-tattle. Rámanáth has had a quarrel with his brother about family matters, and he is not at all averse to doing him a bad turn." Shám Babu was not satisfied with this explanation. He answered:—

"I can hardly believe Rámanáth capable of telling deliberate lies, which must inevitably be detected."

"Perhaps not. It is quite possible that Gopál may be in temporary straits. But can you point to a single merchant among your acquaintances whose career has been uniformly prosperous? There are ups and downs in commerce, which no one can avoid. Mark my words, Gopál will soon pull himself together again!"

Shám Babu was by no means convinced by his brother-in-law's optimism. He remarked, "In any case I ought not to allow my loan to stand without some tangible security. Gopál has house property in Calcutta, I believe?"

"To be sure he has. There is his new house at Entally, which must have cost Rs. 20,000; and another in Barabazar, letting at Rs. 3,000. Just calculate what this property must be worth. If I doubted Gopál's solvency, do you suppose I would have lent him Rs. 20,000 on his note of hand?"

Shám Babu was quite reassured. He came to the conclusion that Rámanáth had attempted to injure his own brother, and returned home with a firm resolve to disregard such scandalous talk in future.

About three months afterwards he met Rámanáth Babu quite casually in Harrison Road and, in the course of conversation, the latter asked whether he had called in his loan to Gopál.

"I have done nothing of the kind," was the curt reply. "My brother-in-law tells me that he is quite solvent."

"It was just like him to say so—the selfish fellow! I am sorry to say that my brother has lost heavily by speculating in jute and is, in fact, a ruined man. If you don't believe me, ask Hari Babu again and you will see what tune he sings. Perhaps you don't know that he has called in his loan of Rs. 20,000?"

"That is certainly strange," replied Shám Babu with tears in his voice. "He never breathed a word of any such intention to me."

"Hari Babu is your brother-in-law," continued Rámanáth, "but Gopál is my own brother. Is it likely that I would injure his reputation gratuitously? No; you are an old friend whom I cannot allow to be ruined without a word of warning. If you do not choose to act upon it, so much the worse for you."

Shám Babu was now convinced that no time was to be lost in demanding proper security for the loan. He went straight to his brother-in-law, to whom he repeated the information which he had received.

Hari Babu shook his head sadly. "Yes," he said, "I am afraid there is some truth in it. Gopál is in temporary difficulties; but you need not be anxious. I will get him to give you a mortgage on landed property worth much more than his debt to you."

Shám Babu felt somewhat reassured, but there was a point to be cleared up.

"One word more," he said, "have you called in your loan of Rs. 20,000?"

Hari Babu looked at him suspiciously. "Who told you so?"

"I heard it from a reliable source."

"It must have been Rámanáth, who is always seeking to make mischief. Well, yes, I did ask Gopál to repay me, not that I distrusted him but because I wanted to invest the money in land."

Shám Babu felt indignant at the man's gross selfishness, but he concealed his feelings and merely remarked that he would not leave Calcutta till the mortgage was settled. Next morning he insisted on Hari Babu accompanying him to Gopál's house at Entally. They found the debtor apparently in high spirits, although he admitted that certain speculations had turned out badly. When pressed by Shám Babu to repay the loan, he asked for time, pleading that his whole capital was locked up. Shám Babu, however, was obdurate, and with his brother-in-law's help he brought such pressure to bear on Gopál that the latter sulkily agreed to give him a mortgage on an ancestral estate in the *Mufassil* (interior of Bengal). Shám Babu stuck closely to him until the bargain had been fulfilled, and managed matters so expeditiously that the mortgage deed was drawn up, executed, and registered in a week. Though he had now something tangible to rely on in case of accidents still he was not happy, for Gopál discontinued paying interest on the loan and he did not dare to press him, lest he should precipitate a crash.

Misfortunes never come singly. Soon after settling this unpleasant affair, Shám Babu was laid low by fever; and doctor's bills trenched sadly on his slender resources. Susil, too, the hope of the family, caught a mysterious disease and was absent from office so long that his employers were obliged to replace him. For the first time in his life, the poor old father felt the pinch of want, but he bore up bravely hoping for better times. When he was able to crawl about again, he applied to his old employers for work of any kind, but learnt to his sorrow that they intended winding up the business and were not able to increase their establishment. Shám Babu scanned the advertisement columns of the daily paper and answered many offers of employment, learning, on each occasion, that he was far too old to fill the coveted post.

One evening he sat in his parlour brooding over the many misfortunes which encompassed him. A distant connection named Srish Babu came in and, hearing that his host sorely needed work, said:—

"I am going to start a business in country produce and shall want several experienced clerks. I must provide for relatives first and strangers afterwards. Now, would you be inclined to come to me as manager, on Rs. 75 a month to begin with?"

Shám Babu jumped at the offer, which would restore him to comparative affluence, and it was agreed that he should enter on his new duties in three weeks. A month passed by without news from his relative, and meantime Shám Babu received a tempting offer of employment. Before deciding what to do he wrote to Srish Babu, informing him of the fact and asking whether he could rely on him. A reply came to the effect that he might do as he pleased, but that the business in country produce, which he was to manage, would positively be started in a fortnight. After another month of suspense, Shám Babu learnt that Srish's bubble had been pricked, and that he had levanted, no one knew whither, to escape a swarm of creditors.

The poor old man was now on his beam-ends. The only course open to him was to sue Gopál for arrears of interest and foreclose his mortgage. After a year and a half's attendance in divers civil courts and spending his last rupee on lawyers' fees, he obtained a decree. When, however, he tried to execute it, it turned out that the estate on which he had a lien was a joint family possession, with the shares so inextricably mixed up that he could neither trace the property mortgaged to him nor discover who was liable for the proportion of profit derived from it. As well poke one's fingers into a hornet's nest as into a joint family estate! Shám Babu was glad to accept an offer of Rs. 5,000 from Gopál's co-sharers, in return for a surrender of his claims. Despite his heavy loss, enough remained to preserve him from penury; and he was even able to start Susil in a small way of business. Great is the virtue of economy!

A PEACEMAKER.

Young Samarendra Dass of Calcutta hoped to enter Government service as a Sub-Deputy Magistrate; but this ambition was thwarted by the sudden decease of his father, who left a widow and two sons entirely unprovided for. After dutifully performing the *srádh* (funeral rites), he waited on the dead man's uncle, Rashbehári Babu by name, with a request that he would support the little family until the sons were in a position to do so. No good Hindu in comfortable circumstances ever turns a deaf ear to such appeals. Rashbehári Babu at once invited the trio to take up their abode with him. Having no nearer relatives, he had resolved to leave his whole fortune to Samarendra and his brother Nagendra; and long before his nephew's death he had executed a will to that effect, which for obvious reasons was kept a profound secret. The young men were, therefore, ignorant of the brilliant prospects in store for them, and worked hard to prepare themselves for earning a livelihood. Samarendra was soon provided with a post as clerk, which yielded enough to provide the cost of his father's funeral ceremony and also enabled him to pay Nagendra's school fees.

One evening Rashbehári Babu went to bed supperless, complaining of indisposition. At midnight, Samarendra was awakened by his groans and found him writhing in agony on the floor. A doctor was summoned in hot haste; but ere his arrival the poor old man had expired in Samarendra's arms. His case was diagnosed as one of failure of the heart's action.

Samarendra and his mother were prostrated by this sudden calamity; but there is no time to be lost in hot weather. Calling in three or four neighbours, they had the body carried to Nimtala Ghat for cremation. Sufficient money was given to the *Muchis* (low-caste men who serve as undertakers) for purchasing an abundant supply of fuel and *ghi* (clarified butter) with which a *chilla* (pyre) was constructed. After the corpse had been laid reverently thereon, Samarendra performed *Mukhagni* ("putting fire in its mouth," the duty of the eldest son or nearest relative). Fire was then applied on four sides, and when the body had been reduced to ashes, Samarendra bathed in the Ganges with his companions, and returned home with wet clothes, shouting "Haribol!" (a cry used at funerals).

Next day Samarendra discovered the dead man's keys, one of which opened a drawer where Rashbehári Babu kept his private papers. Among them was a will, which made himself and his brother sole heirs to the deceased's estate. He ran with the glad news to his mother, who, in the exuberance of her joy, vowed to offer a sumptuous *pujá* at Kali Ghát temple after the *srádh* had been duly performed.

Rashbehári Babu left landed property yielding an annual income of Rs. 1,200, besides Rs. 10,000 deposited in a Calcutta bank, and a substantial house. His estate was worth not less than Rs. 40,000—a lucky windfall for the penniless brothers. It is needless to add that the testator's *srádh* was celebrated with great pomp, which over, Samarendra applied for and obtained probate of the will. A sudden change from dependence to comparative wealth is trying to the best-balanced character. Samarendra's head was turned by the accession of fortune; he began to give himself airs in dealing with acquaintances, and was not over-kind to his mother, who bore her sufferings patiently.

A landed proprietor holds service in contempt. Samarendra at once resigned his post and settled down at Ratnapur, where Rashbehári Babu had owned a house and the bulk of his estate was situated. Soon afterwards he yielded to the repeated advice of his mother by marrying the daughter of a caste-fellow, endowed with goods on a par with her husband's new position.

His brother Nagendra passed the Entrance Examination, but failed to secure a First Arts certificate. This rebuff so disheartened him that he gave up all idea of continuing the University course and returned to Ratnapur with the intention of living in idleness on his property. In vain did Samarendra point out the advantages of a degree. Nagendra declared that such distinctions were beyond his reach. Sudden wealth, in fact, was injurious to both of them.

Two uneventful years passed away. Samarendra's wife was the mother of an idolised boy and was herself adored by her mother-in-law, who never allowed her to do any manner of household work. The result was that her temper changed for the worse. When the old lady fell ill, the young one made horrible messes of her curry and rice. If her husband ventured to remonstrate, she silenced him with abuse, and even emphasised her remarks with a broomstick.

Samarendra, in fact, was completely under his wife's thumb. Her word was law in the household; her mother-in-law a mere cypher, who found both husband and wife perpetually leagued against her. Shortly after his arrival at Ratnapur, Nagendra espoused the daughter of Kanto Babu, a Zemindar residing in the neighbourhood. At first Samarendra's wife received the new-comer graciously enough; but finding that she was of a submissive disposition, she soon began to lord it over her sister-in-law. Nagendra sympathised heartily with his young wife, but had such a horror of family quarrels that he was very loath to intervene on her behalf. One evening, however, he ventured on a word of reproof, which was received with angry words and threats of his eldest brother's vengeance.

Next day Samarendra called him into the parlour, and, after they were seated, said: "I hear you have been rude to *Barabau* (the elder wife). Is that so?"

Nagendra raised his hands in wonder. "No, brother, it was she who showed disrespect to me, simply because I objected to her bullying my wife."

"Do you mean to say that *Barabau* has lied?" thundered Samarendra. His brother was nettled by the tone adopted. He replied hotly, "Yes, she has lied!"

"What!" asked Samarendra beside himself with indignation. "Is my wife a liar and are you a Judisthir?" (the elder of the five Pandav brothers, heroes of the

Mahabharata). "You are a creature without shame!" So saying, he shook his fist at Nagendra who started from his seat as if to attack him. Luckily a respectable neighbour came in at the very nick of time and separated the would-be combatants.

On the morrow, Nagendra told his brother curtly that these perpetual bickerings must be avoided at all cost, and that the only course open to them was to separate. Samarendra raised not the slightest objection, and from that day forward two distinct establishments were set up in the same house. It only remained to divide the estates equally, and as a preliminary step Nagendra asked for accounts during the last three years. They were furnished in a few weeks, and he spent several nights in examining them carefully, taking lists of defaulters in order to verify them by independent inquiry.

While returning home, one evening, from supper at a friend's house, he met a Mohammadan ryot who, according to the accounts, was heavily in arrears of rent. He paused and, after acknowledging the man's salám, remarked that he ought to make an effort to pay a part at least of what was due. The ryot stood aghast with surprise, but invoked Allah to witness that he had paid up every pice, adding that he held *Dákhilas* (rent receipts) from *Bara Babu* (the elder brother) which would prove his assertion. Nagendra asked him to call next day with the receipts in question.

When the man presented himself, Nagendra, in his brother's presence, asked for the arrears of rent shown in the *jamá wásil báqi* (accounts). Again the ryot affirmed that he owned nothing and appealed to the *Bara Babu* for corroboration. Samarendra was taken aback.

"Yes," he stammered, "you did pay me something about a month ago."

"Why do you say 'something,' Babu? You know quite well that I discharged my rent in full; and what is more I have receipts." So saying he untied a knot in his *gamcha* (wrapper) and extracted some greasy papers, which he flourished in Samarendra's face, shouting, "Will you swear by your gods that these are not in your writing?"

Nagendra took the receipts, which bore his brother's signature. The latter looked somewhat sheepish as he answered: "My memory failed me; I now recollect receiving our rent from you."

Nagendra turned sharply on his brother with the question: "Then why did you not enter these receipts in your *karcha* (cash-book)?"

"I'm sure I don't know," was the reply; "probably I forgot to do so."

Though Nagendra said nothing at the time, his doubts of Samarendra's probity became certainties. From that day onward he was indefatigable in studying the copy of the *siah* (rent-roll) furnished him, the cash-book, and statement of arrears. Figures set down in these accounts were checked by private inquiries among the ryots themselves. Then the truth dawned on Nagendra, that his brother had misappropriated large sums, which should have been paid to him, and concealed his fraud by falsifying the Zemindari papers. After preparing a list of defalcations, he showed it to his brother and asked for an explanation. None was forthcoming; nay, Samarendra made his case worse by flying into a passion and ordering him out of the room. He went straight to Kanto Babu for advice, and was told that the only course open to him was to sue his brother for recovery of the amount wrongfully appropriated. He resolved to do so forthwith.

On the self-same night his wife, after discussing household affairs with him as usual, asked casually why he had paid her father a visit. He told her everything that occurred without reserve. The young lady listened with breathless attention, but heaved a deep sigh on learning that he intended suing his elder brother. Nagendra paused and asked what was on her mind.

"My lord," was her reply, "I am only a woman, knowing nothing of the world except things within my sphere. Any attempt on my part to meddle in business matters may seem extremely presumptuous. But this is such a grave and risky matter that I cannot help speaking out. If you file a suit against your brother, he will of course defend himself; for to lose it would ruin him in purse and honour. It will drag on for months. If you get a decree, the defendant will appeal to the Sub-Judge, and eventually to the High Court. To fight your way step by step will cost a fortune; and even should you win all along the line, the lawyers will not leave you enough to keep body and soul together. How can a small estate like yours bear the costs of both sides? So in my humble opinion it would be much better to allow your brother to enjoy his ill-gotten gains. Make up your mind, from this day forward, to look carefully after your interests, and you may rest assured that your brother will never try any such tricks again."

Nagendra listened with open mouth to this discourse, and when his wife had done speaking, he embraced her fondly again and again, murmuring:—

"My dearest love, I never knew your real worth till now. The Goddess of Wisdom has chosen you as her messenger and has convinced me that lawsuits are luxuries which only the rich folk can enjoy—not people in my position. I will certainly see your father to-morrow and tell him my resolve to take no steps whatever against Samarendra."

A Hindu wife is her husband's truest friend; ever eager to share his sorrows and to proffer sound advice in times of difficulty. Yet these sweet, unselfish creatures are systematically libelled by men who owe everything to them. It was soon noised abroad that Nagendra's wife had saved him from inevitable ruin. Everyone praised her common-sense—not excepting Samarendra and his wife, who thenceforward treated her with more consideration. Nagendra, therefore, began to hope that peace and unity would again rule the family.

A BRAHMAN'S CURSE.

Despite his lack of training Samarendra Babu had great capacities for business, and seldom lost a chance of profit-making. He saw that people around him stood in constant need of funds to defray the cost of religious and family rites, and were ready to pay 60 per cent. for loans—at least they undertook to do so. It occurred to him that if he lent money on unimpeachable security at something under the market rates, he could not fail to make a large fortune. Soon after he had set up as a banker, the neighbours flocked to him for advances, which he granted only to such as could offer substantial security; his charges by way of interest being 30 to 40 per cent. He also started a business in lending ryots rice for their seed-grain and support till the harvest should be reaped. It is needless to add that his clients paid heavily for this accommodation. So rapidly did his dealings increase that he sought an agent to represent him at the district headquarters; and particularly to buy up defaulters' estates at the auctions which are held periodically under Government auspices. His choice fell upon one Bipinbehári Bhur, who had a widespread reputation for acuteness. It was not belied. In less than a year Bipin had secured for his master estates yielding a net income of nearly Rs. 1,200, which had cost a mere song at auction. Samarendra Babu never failed to reward him for such bargains. On one occasion he had such a slice of luck that it is worth while to narrate it in some detail.

He had just retired to rest for the night, when a servant knocked at the door to say that Bipin had come on very urgent business. Samarendra Babu went downstairs to his parlour, clad in a wrapper, to find his agent pacing up and down in evident agitation. After the usual compliments had been exchanged, he asked why Bipin had called so late.

"I have bad news for you, Mahásay," was the reply. "You remember buying the Shibprakásh estate at last auction? Well, that property may slip through your fingers." He paused to watch the effect of the announcement on his master, and then went on: "The late proprietor has lodged an objection to its sale, on the ground that no arrears were due, producing a receipt to substantiate his contention. The Collector has just called on us to show cause against the cancellation of the sale and will take the case up the day after to-morrow."

Samarendra was thunderstruck by this information, the Shibprakásh estate being one of the best bargains he had ever got. After pondering a while, he asked, "What would you advise me to do? I am afraid it is hopeless to contend against a receipt in full!"

Bipin was not so easily disheartened. He replied, "Let us consult our pleader,

Asu Babu, who is sure to have some plan for upholding the sale. He won't ask more than Rs. 100, which is not a tenth of the annual profits for Shibprakásh." This course commended itself to Samarendra, who sent his headman back to Ghoria, promising to follow next day, with the necessary sinews of war. He arrived betimes at Bipin's house there, and took him to the Bar Library, where Asu Babu was sure to be found when not engaged in Court. A few minutes later the limb of the law came in, and asked what business brought Samarendra to Ghoria.

After hearing the story of Shibprakásh and its vicissitudes of ownership, he asked:—

"How much will you pay me if I win your case?"

Glancing at Bipin, Samarendra answered hesitatingly, "Well, I might go as far as fifty rupees".

"Nonsense," was the rejoinder. "I won't take a pice less than Rs. 100." After several minutes wasted on haggling, it was agreed that Asu Babu should be paid Rs. 40 on the nail and Rs. 35 more if he won the suit. The pleader pocketed this first instalment, and assured Samarendra that he would prove the sale to have been perfectly valid. Then the trio separated, Samarendra returning to Bipin's house where they passed the day in forming plans for further purchases.

At 10.30 on the morrow, both attended at the Collectorate and found that the Shibprakásh objection stood first for hearing. It was opened by the appellant's pleader, who rose armed with a huge account book and bundle of receipts, in order to prove that his client owed nothing to Government, and that the sale proceedings were a blunder from beginning to end. Asu Babu waited till his turn came, and then informed the Collector that he would find, on examining his books, that the appellant was Rs. 1 11. 0. in arrears at the date of the sale. The Collector ordered his head clerk to produce the ledger account of payments on account of the Shibprakásh estates, and, sure enough, they showed a short payment of the amount stated. This was a thunderbolt for the appellant, whose pleader vainly tried to pick holes in the accounts, but was at last obliged to confess that a mistake had been made. The only course open to him was to sue for mercy. The Collector, however, was inexorable, and indeed he had no power to mitigate the Draconian law of sale. That of Shibprakásh was duly confirmed, and its new owner adjourned to the bar library to settle matters with his pleader. The meeting was joyful indeed. After congratulating Asu Babu on his unexpected success, Samarendra asked how he had managed it. The pleader at first refused to gratify his curiosity, but yielded to entreaty. "The tiger has a jackal," he said, "and I, who cannot stoop to dirty tricks myself, have a certain *mukhtiár* (the lowest grade of advocates) who is hand-in-glove with all the *amlas* (clerks) and can twist them round his finger—for a consideration. I gave him Rs. 10 out of the advance money and promised as much more if he could persuade the Collectorate clerks to cook the appellant's accounts, so as to show a short payment. You see how well he has succeeded, and now I think the least you can do is to refund the douceur to me." Samarendra agreed and handed Asu Babu Rs. 55, prophesying that he would have a brilliant career at the bar.

He had to stop for a fortnight or so at Ghoria, in order to get possession of his purchase from the Collectorate *názir* (bailiff) who, according to custom, planted a bamboo thereon, as a symbol of its transfer. While waiting for this formality he attended another sale for arrears of revenue, in the hope of picking up some profitable bargains. He was not disappointed. The last lot was the whole of Jayrámpur, a small village quite close to his house, inhabited by hardworking and submissive ryots, who paid their rent punctually. Samarendra was all agog when the názir read out the names of its proprietors, the amount of arrears, and the boundaries, calling on the crowd to bid. A dead silence followed, which was at last broken by a timid offer of Rs. 1,000. Samarendra promptly bid Rs. 6,000, which he knew was hardly three years' purchase of the net rental, and the rise was so tremendous that it choked off all competition. Jayrámpur was knocked down to him; but his exultation was tempered by the discovery that he had not nearly enough to meet the amount of earnest money which had to be paid down at once. A *mukhtiár* came to his aid by whispering offers of a loan, and the requisite amount was forthcoming in five minutes, on Samarendra's giving his note of hand with a bonus of 10 per cent. payable next day.

His star continued to be in the eleventh heaven; for this was one of a series of profitable purchases. In seven or eight years he owned estates yielding an income of Rs. 8,000, while his dealings in grain produced half as much again.

Samarendra's ambition rose with growing prosperity. Visions of a title hovered in his brain, and being a man of resource, he hit upon an ingenious method of converting them into realities. Close to his house there was an extensive *bil* (marsh) peopled in season by swarms of wild-duck, teal and snipe. It was visited occasionally by Europeans from Calcutta, who are always on the alert for a day's sport, but they were inconvenienced by the total lack of accommodation. So Samarendra built a neat bungalow, equipped it with European furniture, and placed an old *Khánsámá* (Mohammadan butler) in charge, who was versed in all the customs of *Sáheb-log* (Englishmen). This menial had orders to report the arrival of white visitors and offer them hospitality. His courtesy was highly appreciated, and there was scarcely a Sunday during the cold weather which did not bring a couple of sportsmen to the bungalow. Samarendra attended personally to their comforts, thus making many friends. Through their influence he secured *carte blanche* in the matter of guns and ammunition—a boon which seldom falls to the lot of middle-class Indians. At their request he subscribed to various European clubs, winning the reputation of being "not half a bad sort of fellow". All this hospitality, however, was terribly expensive, and it soon exceeded Samarendra's income. But he went on spending money like water, in the assurance that one day it would yield a golden return.

On a bright morning, in January, 18—, he was sitting in his bungalow, in the hope of welcoming guests, when a European entered it, attended by two orderlies; and seeing a well-dressed Indian, was about to retire. Samarendra introduced himself as the local Zemindar and offered to send a *shikári* (game-keeper) with the visitor in order to show him some sport. His overtures were gratefully received, and the European, on returning at noon with a heavy bag, was delighted to find an appetising tiffin ready for his acceptance. Samarendra kept out of the way until it was finished, and then asked whether his guest had enjoyed himself. The latter was profuse in thanks and, ere leaving for the neighbouring railway station, asked whether he could be of any service, tendering a card inscribed, "Mr. Charles Bernardson, Indian Civil Service." He was none other than the Chief Secretary to Government.

Such an acquaintance was not to be lost sight of. A week later Samarendra went to Calcutta and called on Mr. Bernardson at his chambers in the United Service Club. He was received, so to speak, with open arms, questioned about crops, crime, sport, and other commonplace topics, and again assured that Mr. Bernardson would serve him in any way within his power. The latter hint was promptly taken. On receiving permission to quit the great man's presence he timidly suggested that he would like to be an Honorary Magistrate. Mr. Bernardson took note of the wish, and a few weeks later the *Gazette* announced Samarendra's nomination to the Ghoria Independent Bench, with power to try cases singly.

The next point was to attract the attention of the district authorities. Samarendra pored over the Penal and Procedure Codes, took lessons in law from Asu Babu, and soon mastered the routine of a petty Court of Justice. He never missed any sitting of the Bench and signalised himself by a rigorous interpretation of the law. Offenders had short shrift from him; and the police moved heaven and earth to get their cases disposed of in his Court. His percentage of convictions was larger than that of any honorary magistrate. Such zeal deserved a suitable reward, and it soon attracted the attention of the authorities. On New Year's Day, 189–, the *Calcutta Gazette* came out with its usual list of honours, amongst which was seen a Rái Bahádurship for Samarendra. This dignity answers to the English knighthood, and it is usually made an excuse for rejoicings shared by all classes. Samarendra, however, thought it unnecessary to waste money on junketings. He preferred subscribing to movements favoured by the "little tin gods" of Darjiling.

Towards the end of the same year, he was accosted, while leaving Court one afternoon, by a *chuprássi* (orderly) attached to the magistrate-collector's person, who salámed obsequiously and said that the *Bara Saheb* wished to see him at once. Hastening to the district chief's bungalow he was graciously received, and in the course of conversation a remark fell from the great man's lips, which made the blood course wildly through his veins. It seemed that a fund had been started in Calcutta for the purpose of erecting some permanent memorial to the late Viceroy, and a hint was thrown out that if Samarendra subscribed liberally, he might possibly find himself gazetted a "Rájá Bahádur". He assured the magistrate that the Memorial Fund would receive a handsome donation from him and asked for a few days in order to decide the amount.

On returning home, he made a rough calculation of his assets and liabilities. The latter amounted to nearly a lakh of rupees (£6,666), or about five times his net annual income. Common prudence suggested that he ought not to increase the burden; but ambition prevailed, and the only question which Samarendra set himself was, "What is the least amount I can decently give?" After thinking over pros and cons for a whole night, he decided that Rs. 10,000 would be enough; raised that sum at 12 per cent, by mortgaging some landed property, and sent it with a flowery letter to the District Magistrate, as a humble donation to the Viceroy's Memorial Fund.

A few days later Samarendra was preparing for a visit to his favourite rest-house, in the vague hope that Mr. Bernardson might turn up again, when a strange Brahman entered the courtyard and thus addressed him:—

"Sir, you are an Amir, and I am a beggar. I have a request to make."

"Cut it short," replied Samarendra testily. "Come to the point—what do you want?"

"Sir, I have a grown-up daughter who positively must be married; but I cannot raise a sufficient dowry. Will your honour give me a trifle towards making one up?"

"No, I won't; if you belonged to this village you would know that I cannot afford to fling money about. My expenses are enormous!"

"Now, please, don't refuse me, Rái Bahádur; surely you can spare a couple of rupees to a poor Brahman!"

Samarendra was exasperated by the man's importunity. He replied sharply, "You and your kind seem to think that I am *Kuver* (the God of Wealth) incarnate, who is able to satisfy every human need! I won't give you anything!"

"Only one rupee, Rái Bahádur," pleaded the Brahman with folded hands.

"No! no! Get out of my house at once!" bellowed Samarendra; then turning to his doorkeeper, he ordered him to "run the fellow out of the yard by the neck."

The Brahman was deeply incensed. Drawing himself up to his full height, he looked scornfully at Samarendra, and said:—

"Babu, you dare to order me, a Brahman, to be ejected with violence from your house. Is there no religion left in this world? Mark my words, a day is coming when you will be poorer even than myself. I have spoken." Then he strode out of the courtyard in high dudgeon. Samarendra merely laughed aloud and hurled mocking epithets after his retreating figure, to which no reply was vouchsafed.

Next morning he received a letter from the District Magistrate which filled him with mingled joy and terror. It contained a curt request to call at once on a matter of great importance. He drove to the great man's bungalow arrayed in his best, but was kept waiting for nearly a quarter of an hour in the porch. When he was ushered into the magistrate's study he saw intuitively that something was wrong. His salám was returned by a mere inclination of the head and a request to be seated. Then the Magistrate spoke in tones of chilling politeness:—

"Rái Bahádur, I've sent for you to say that a subscription of Rs. 10,000 is wholly unworthy of your position. If you wish, I will send it to the Secretary of the Memorial Fund; but I warn you plainly that the most you can expect in return is an expression of the Lieutenant-Governor's thanks in the *Gazette*. I could not possibly recommend you for a title for such a paltry sum."

Poor Samarendra's heart beat more loudly than the clock on the magistrate's mantelpiece. He stammered out: "I need only assure your honour that I have given as much as I could afford; but if your honour thinks the amount insufficient—er—er—er—I am quite willing to give—twice as much". So saying he awaited a reply in trembling apprehension. It was satisfactory.

"Now, Rái Bahádur, you are talking sense. Send me Rs. 10,000 more for the fund and I'll undertake to submit your name to Government for a Rájáship. It will be just in time for the New Year's *Gazette*. Now you may take leave."

Samarendra bowed himself out with precipitation and, on returning home, sent for his factotum, Bipin, to whom he related this momentous interview, with an injunction to raise Rs. 10,000 more by hook or by crook. Bipin shook his head ominously and feared that no moneylender would advance any considerable sum on estates already over-burdened. However, he promised to do his best and negotiated so successfully that Rs. 10,000 were procured at 24 per cent. in less than a week. This additional subscription was gracefully acknowledged by the District Magistrate, and a fortnight later Samarendra's drooping spirits were revived by the appearance of a notification in the *Gazette* thanking him warmly for his "munificence and public spirit". There was nothing for it but to count the days of the expiring year.

On 31st December, 189-, his impatience could brook no further delay. Hurrying to Calcutta by train, he sent a trusty servant to the Government printing office with orders to obtain the earliest copy of the *Gazette* at any price. He slept not a wink on that fateful night and rose betimes to intercept the messenger.

At last the bulky document was thrust into his hands. He unfolded it with trembling fingers and glanced downwards through an interminable list of newly-made Máhárájas, Nawáb Bahádurs, Rájá Bahádurs, and Rájás—in the hope of finding his own name. Alas, it was conspicuous by its absence. Oh, the pangs of hope deferred and wounded pride! Death seemed to Samarendra preferable to a life of poverty and despair. He returned home crestfallen and nursed his disappointment until it landed him in a severe attack of brain fever. As soon as he felt strong enough to leave the house, he drove to the magistrate's house for explanation and comfort. He was courteously received, but the Chief hinted that there might be a hitch about the title, as he himself had enemies in the Secretariat, who would be glad of an opportunity of placing him in a false position. He counselled patience and expressed a conviction that the birthday *Gazette* would contain the notification so ardently desired.

This was comforting, but Samarendra resolved to push his own interests. He remembered the promises made by Mr. Bernardson and took the next train to Calcutta in order to secure his influence. On reaching the Secretariat he learnt, with deep annoyance, that Mr. Bernardson had taken sick leave to England and was not likely to return. So the only course open was to wait for 24th May. Again he was disappointed, the list of birthday honours ignoring him completely. Samarendra had not even the resource of consulting the official who had lured him into extravagant expenditure. The District Magistrate was transferred to a distant and unhealthy part of the province, and his successor disclaimed all knowledge of the bargain.

Samarendra's long suspense and repeated disappointments told severely on his health. He neglected business, leaving everything in the hands of Bipin, who was more anxious to feather his own nest than extricate his master from difficulties; so the interest in mortgages fell into arrears. One creditor bolder than the rest sued him and foreclosed; then others were encouraged to attack the ruined man. In less than a year, Samarendra was stripped of every *bigha* (one-third of an acre) of land he once possessed, and attachments galore were issued against his moveable property. Too late did he see the depths of folly into which he had fallen.

Grief and despair brought on a second attack of brain fever, which exhausted his failing strength. After tossing for several weeks in delirium he regained sense only to feel assured that the end of all worldly ambition was fast approaching. Then he remembered the Brahman's curse, and knowing that it was the cause of all his misfortunes he endeavoured to make some reparation; but the holy man was not to be found. One evening he fell into a deep slumber from which he never awoke, leaving a wife and several helpless children in comparative penury. Then a hush fell on the land, and people whispered that *Brahmateja* (the power of Brahmans) was by no means extinct.

A ROLAND FOR HIS OLIVER.

Nagendra's soul was not haunted by any such ambitions. He was content with the surplus profits from his landed estates, which he did not invest in trade or even Government paper, but hoarded in a safe. By slow degrees he amassed a small fortune, and when Samarendra's growing impecuniosity forced him to ask his brother for a loan of Rs. 2,000, it was readily granted on a mere note of hand. In less than six months the borrower died and, after waiting as long, Nagendra pressed his sister-in-law for payment of the debt. She referred him to her brother, Priyanath Guha, who, she said, was manager of what property she had left. This man was a scoundrel of the deepest dye, and Samarendra, who was fully aware of the fact, never allowed him inside the house. After his death Priya made himself so useful to the widow that she invited him to live in her house and trusted him implicitly. When the neighbours learnt this arrangement they whispered that the poor woman would inevitably be reduced to beggary.

Nagendra reluctantly applied to Priya for a refund of the loan, producing Samarendra's note of hand, which was about a year overdue. After examining it, Priya said:—

"The matter is simple enough. My sister must repay you; but you know the muddle in which her husband's affairs were left, and I'm sure you won't refuse to renew the bond."

Nagendra replied that he would gladly give his sister any reasonable time to discharge her debt.

"Very well," rejoined Priya. "What do you say to my renewing this note of hand for six months, with 12 per cent. interest?"

"I have no objection," said Nagendra, "but you must satisfy me first that you hold a general power of attorney to act for her."

"Oh, you doubt my word," sneered Priya, "but I don't blame you; such is the way of the world."

So saying he took a registered power of attorney out of his sister's strong box, which Nagendra saw entitled him to transact any business whatever relating to her estate. He handed the bond to Priya and asked him to endorse the conditions agreed on. While doing so Priya looked up. "Have you any objection," he asked, "to my antedating the renewal a week or so. The fact is, Baisakh 12th has always been a lucky day in my family and I should like to date my endorsement then."

"Just as you like," answered Nagendra indifferently; and after reading the endorsement through very carefully he took the note of hand away without saluting

Priya.

Not hearing from him when the note matured, Nagendra called at his sister's house and pressed Priya, whom he found there, for payment of the Rs. 2,000 and interest.

Priya gazed at him with feigned astonishment. "What loan are you talking about?" he asked.

Nagendra attempted to jog his memory, but he stoutly denied having renewed any note of hand which purported to have been executed by Samarendra. When the document was shown him, he boldly declared that the endorsement was a forgery, and further that the handwriting on the note of hand itself was not Samarendra's. Nagendra stood aghast for awhile and, on regaining his wits, he said, "I ought to have known better than trust a *haramzádá* like you!"

"Now don't descend to personalities," rejoined Priya. "I can prove that the endorsement could not have been executed by me; and the whole transaction looks fishy."

This was too much for Nagendra, who lost his temper and abused the scoundrel roundly. They separated with threats of mutual vengeance.

On the morrow, Nagendra instructed a pleader to file a suit against his sister for recovery of the principal and interest due on the promissory note. When it came on for hearing before the Subordinate Judge, Nagendra Babu was dumbfoundered by hearing the defendant's pleader aver that the endorsement could not possibly be genuine, inasmuch as his client was fifteen hundred miles from Ratnapur at the alleged date of execution. He then placed Priya in the box, to swear that, on Baisakh 12th, he was at Lahore, in order to give evidence in a civil suit. All doubt vanished in the Sub Judge's mind when the pleader handed him a document bearing the seal of the Chief Court of the Punjab, certifying that Priya had been in attendance on that day. He dismissed the suit with costs against Nagendra, and remarked that this palpable forgery cast discredit on the whole transaction.

It was a wise man who said that we hate our enemies less for the harm they have done us than for the harm we have done them. Priya was not content with depriving Nagendra of his dues; he resolved to injure him more materially. About a month after his unlucky lawsuit, Nagendra learnt quite by accident that one of his estates named Lakhimpur had been notified for sale for arrears of land revenue amounting to Rs. 197 odd. The Naib (manager), on being asked to account for this, laid all the blame on the ryots, who, he said, would not be made to pay their rent and thus deprived him of the means of satisfying the Government demand. Nagendra rebuked him for gross negligence and failing to report the matter, for, he added, the arrears would have been paid from his own pocket. He at once dismissed the Naib from his employ and hastened to Ghoria, where he instructed a pleader named Asu Babu to petition the collector for leave to make good the arrears on Lakhimpur. The request was perforce rejected. Lakhimpur was put up for sale and Nagendra ascertained that the purchaser was a man of straw representing Priya himself. He endured the loss of a valuable property, resolving to be even some day with his enemy.

On the following night he was about to retire to bed, when the Lakhimpur Naib burst into the parlour and clasped his master's feet which he bedewed with tears. Nagendra shook him off roughly and asked how he dared to intrude upon him.

"Mahásay," whined the Naib, "I want to make a clean breast of my misdeeds. It was Priya who persuaded me to withhold the revenue due on Lakhimpur, by promising me a reward of Rs. 2,000 if the estate was auctioned. Now that he has got possession of it, he refuses to carry out his bargain and actually offers me Rs. 20, saying that I deserved no more. The black-hearted villain! Now I am come to implore forgiveness of my sin and to make amends for it."

Nagendra was amazed by the fellow's villainy and impudence. He reflected, however, that nothing was to be gained by kicking him out of the house, while his offer of reparation was not to be despised. He replied, "You have been faithless to your salt; but I will pardon you on one condition that you help me to regain my estate, lost through your treachery."

"That I will," protested the Naib. "Only let me have Rs. 300 in currency notes of one hundred rupees each, previously recording the numbers. I swear by Mother Káli, not only to pay the arrears of revenue but to get the sale quashed." Nagendra at first thought that to do so would be only throwing good money after bad; but the man was terribly in earnest, and evidently hostile to their common enemy. He opened his safe and handed the Naib the amount he asked, after carefully taking the numbers of the notes.

At the same hour on the morrow, the Naib returned in high glee to say that the business had been satisfactorily concluded. All Nagendra had to do was to file a petition praying for the cancellation of the sale, and it could not fail to be granted. On being asked how he had contrived to evade the law, the Naib went on:—

"I will tell you the whole truth, Mahásay, only concealing names; for the people, who helped me extracted an oath that I would keep them a profound secret. I went straight from your house last night to that of an office tout, who is a precious rascal, but tolerated because he is in some way related to the Collectorate head clerk. On hearing my story he said he thought the matter could be settled, and asked me to meet him at 1 P.M. under a Nim tree north of the Collectorate, when he would bring a man to me who was able to do all we wished. I was punctual to the minute, and sure enough the tout came with one of the Collectorate clerks. I asked him whether it would not be possible so to manipulate the accounts of Lakhimpur, as to show that all Government revenue had been paid prior to the alleged default. The clerk at first refused to have hand in such a transaction, as it would be too risky; but when I produced my currency notes he thought the job might be attempted, and added that some of the Treasury *amlas* (clerks) would have to be squared as well as himself. I thereupon handed him Rs. 300, saying that it was enough to discharge the revenue due on Lakhimpur and leave more than Rs. 100 to divide as *bakshish* (gratuity). He said that he would do his best and made me swear never to divulge his name. We then separated, and only two hours ago the tout came to my house with the news that the accounts had been corrected."

Nagendra was delighted on hearing these clever tactics and straightway ordered his pleader, Asutosh Sen, widely known as Asu Babu, to file a petition praying for the cancellation of the sale. It came in due course before the Collector for hearing. He called for the accounts, which fully substantiated the petitioner's statements. After hearing the arguments of Priya's representative the Collector said that he was fully satisfied that a mistake had been made, and called on the head clerk to explain the non-entry of a payment made before the due date. That officer laid the whole blame on an unfortunate apprentice, who was promptly dismissed. The sale was declared null and void, and Nagendra regained his own to the intense disgust of the rascally Priya.

RÁMDÁ.

Nagendra Babu was now the wealthiest man in Ratnapur. Puffed up by worldly success, he began to treat his neighbours arrogantly and, with one exception, they did not dare to pay him back in his own coin. Rámdás Ghosal, known far and wide as Rámdá, flattered or feared no one. Having a little rent-free and inherited land, he was quite independent of patronage. Rámdá was "everyone's grandfather," a friend of the poor, whose joys and sorrows he shared. He watched by sick-beds, helped to carry dead bodies to the burning-ghát, in short did everything in his power for others, refusing remuneration in any shape. He was consequently loved and respected by all classes. Rámdá was the consistent enemy of hypocrisy and oppression—qualities which became conspicuous in Nagendra Babu's nature under the deteriorating influence of wealth. He met the great man's studied insolence with a volley of chaff, which is particularly galling to vain people because they are incapable of understanding it.

Nagendra Babu did not forget the Brahman's presumption and determined to teach him a lesson. So, one day, he sent him a written notice demanding the immediate payment of arrears of rent due for a few *bighas* (one-third of an acre) of land which Rámdá held on a heritable lease. As luck would have it the crops had failed miserably, and Rámdá was unable to discharge his debts. On receiving a more peremptory demand seven days later, he called on Nagendra Babu, whom he thus addressed:—

"Why, Nagen, what's the matter with you? You are plaguing me to death with notices, yet you must be aware that I can't pay you a pice at present."

"Thákur," replied Nagendra Babu in stern accents, "I will listen to none of your excuses. Do you mean to tell me that you decline to discharge your arrears?"

"I never said that," protested Rámdá; "but you must really wait till the beginning of next year. My cold weather crops are looking well; and—"

"No, that won't do at all. If you do not pay up in a week, I will certainly have recourse to the civil court."

"Do so by all means if your sense of religion permits," rejoined Rámdá, leaving the parlour in smothered wrath.

When the week of grace had expired, Nagendra Babu filed a suit in the local Múnsiffs Court against his defaulter. As soon as the fact was bruited abroad a universal protest was roused against Nagendra Babu's harshness. Some of the village elders remonstrated with him, but were told to mind their own business; whereon they laid their heads together and subscribed the small sum due from the Brahman. A deputation of five waited on him with entreaties to accept it, but he refused to take the money on any other footing than a loan. So Rámdá paid his arrears and costs into Court, to the plaintiff's intense annoyance.

Samarendra Babu had left his wife and children in comparatively poor circumstances; for, after discharging his debts, they had barely Rs. 300 a year to live on. The widow declined to seek Nagendra Babu's help, even if she were reduced to beg in the streets. After her brother's imprisonment, she had no one to manage her little property which, as a Purdanashin (lit. "one sitting behind the veil"), she was unable to do herself. After mature reflection she sent for Rámdá, who had known her from infancy. He obeyed the summons with alacrity and gave the poor woman sound advice regarding the direction of the Zemindary. By acting on it she was able to increase her income and live in tolerable comfort. Observing that Rámdá was a frequent visitor, Nagendra Babu hinted to his sister-in-law that, if she cared for her reputation, she would not be so thick with him. She flared up instantly. "I will talk to any of my friends I please," said she, "and you shan't poke your nose into my affairs!"

"Very well," replied Nagendra angrily, "but you may rely on my making it hot for that old scoundrel shortly!"

This threat was of course repeated to Rámdá, who merely laughed. As far as he was concerned Nagendra might act as he pleased.

A few days afterwards the bailiff of Nagendra Babu's estate, known as Lakhimpur, called on Rámdá with a verbal request that he should surrender his ancestral tenure and, meeting with a curt refusal, left the house threatening all sorts of evil consequences. Next day, indeed, Rámdá received a notice from Nagendra Babu, calling on him to show cause against the cancellation of his lease on the ground that, by mismanaging the land, he had rendered it unfit for cultivation. Rámdá called some of his neighbours together, to whom he exhibited the document. They expressed the greatest indignation and assured him that they would spend their last rupee in defending his interests. Rámdá gave them a heartfelt blessing and promised a divine reward for their sympathy.

Calling on Samarendra's widow the same day, he was distressed to find that she had received a similar notice, which aimed at robbing her of a small estate, on the ground that it had been surrendered by her husband in part payment of his debt to Nagendra Babu. She knew nothing of any such arrangement and assured Rámdá that, if the property was lost, her income would fall to little more than Rs. 100, meaning starvation for herself and little ones. Her trusty counsellor told her not to lose heart, for she might rely on his help.

In due course the suit against Rámdá came on for hearing before the Munsiff. His pleader established by documentary evidence that the tenure was one without any condition whatever; while the neighbours came forward to prove that the land in dispute had been admirably tilled. The plaintiff, therefore, was non-suited, with costs. The very same result attended Nagendra Babu's action against his sister-in-law, whose case excited universal sympathy. He lost heavily in purse and left the Court with a ruined reputation. It was natural that a man so evil-minded should regard Rámdá as the author of misfortunes due to his own wicked nature. He plotted the poor Brahman's destruction, but no effectual means of compassing it suggested itself.

As days and weeks wore on, his despondency became deeper and, one evening, while sitting with the Lakhimpur bailiff, he asked whether there was any remedy which would restore his peace of mind. The cunning rascal said nothing at the time; but at a late hour on the morrow he came to Nagendra Babu's house with a large bottle hidden under his wrapper. It contained some light brown fluid, which the bailiff poured into a tumbler. Then adding a small quantity of water, he invited his master to swallow the mixture. A few minutes after doing so, the patient was delighted to find that gloomy thoughts disappeared as if by magic. An unwonted elation of spirits succeeded; he broke into snatches of song, to the intense surprise of the household! His amateur physician left the bottle, advising him to take a similar dose every night; and Nagendra Babu followed the prescription punctiliously, with the best effect on his views of life. After finishing the bottle he asked for another, which was brought to him secretly. It had a showy label reading, "Exshaw No. 1 Cognac". Nagendra Babu's conscience accused him of disobeying the Shástras; but the die was cast. He could no longer exist without a daily dose of the subtle poison; and gradually increased it to a tumblerful, forgetting to add water.

His faithful wife did her best to wean him from the fatal habit. She even ventured to abstract his brandy bottle and dilute its contents. On being detected, she underwent a personal correction which was not soon forgotten. The poor creature, indeed, underwent every sort of humiliation from her worthless husband, which she bore in silence, hoping that time would bring him to his senses.

Drunken men are proverbially cunning. After brooding long over his supposed grievances Nagendra matured a scheme of revenge. He intercepted Rámdá, one afternoon, on his way to visit Samarendra's widow, and, affecting sincere penitence for the injury he had endeavoured to work, he invited the unsuspecting Brahman into his sitting-room. Once inside, he suddenly thrust a brass vessel into his visitor's hand and dragged him into the yard, shouting "Thief! thief!" The Lakhimpur bailiff, who was sitting on the verandah, also laid hands on Rámdá and, with the aid of two up-country servants, he was dragged to the police station, too bewildered to resist. On their way thither they met one of Nagendra's neighbours named Harish Chandra Pál, who stopped them and asked what was the matter. On learning particulars of the charge, he saw how the land lay, and resolved to defeat an infamous plot. So waiting till the little crowd was out of sight, he ran back to Nagendra's house and whispered to him that the bailiff had sent for more property, in order that the case against Rámdá might look blacker. Nagendra handed him a fine muslin shawl and loin-cloth, and a set of gold buttons, adding that he would follow in half an hour in order to depose against the thief. On reaching the police station, Harish found the Sub-Inspector recording the statements of the witnesses. He looked on in silence until Nagendra arrived. Then he asked the Sub-Inspector: "Do these people mean to say that the brass vessel belongs to Nagendra Babu?"

"Certainly," was the reply. "Here are three witnesses who have identified it."

"Well, that's strange," said Harish; then producing the shawl and loin-cloth he said: "These are mine, but if you ask Nagen Babu he will tell you a different story".

"But they are mine!" roared Nagendra, "and part of the stolen property."

"Dear me," said Harish, "perhaps you will say that these buttons are yours too?"

"Of course they are," was the rejoinder.

"Now, Sub-Inspector Babu," said Harish, "you must see that Nagendra Babu is subject to strange hallucinations since he has taken to drink. He fancies that he is the god of wealth personified, and that everything belongs to him. I am quite certain that Rámdá has been falsely charged with stealing a brass vessel which is his own property."

The Sub-Inspector evidently thought so too. He called the prosecutor into an inner room. What passed between them there was never known; but presently the Sub-Inspector returned to the office and ordered the prisoner to be at once released. Rámdá was truly grateful to Harish Pál for having so cleverly saved him from ruin, and the whole story soon became common property. Nagendra overheard his neighbours whispering and pointing to him significantly, and village boys called him ill-natured nicknames in the street. His irritation was increased by recourse to the brandy bottle, and he vented it on his luckless wife. She suffered so terribly that, one morning, Nagendra found her hanging from a rafter in his cowshed. This suicide was the last straw. Nagendra saved himself from prosecution for murder by a heavy bribe, and got leave from the police to burn his wife's body. But so universally was he execrated that not a man in the village would help him to take her body to the burning-ghát. In dire despair he humbled himself so far as to implore Rámdá's assistance. The magnanimous Brahman forgot his wrongs and cheerfully consented to bear a hand. Others followed his example, and thus Nagendra was able to fulfil the rites prescribed by religion. The lesson was not altogether lost on him. The scales fell from his eyes; he dismissed the rascally servant, who had led him from the path of duty, and foreswore his brandy bottle.

A RIFT IN THE LUTE.

Nalini Chandra Basu worked hard for the B.L. degree, not to fill his pockets by juggling with other people's interests, but in order to help the poor, who are so often victims of moneyed oppression. After securing the coveted distinction, he was enrolled as a pleader of the Calcutta High Court and began to practise there, making it a rule to accept no fees from an impoverished client. But two years of constant attendance at Court convinced Nalini that Calcutta had far too many lawyers already. He therefore removed to Ghoria, knowing that he would find plenty of wrongs to redress there. About a month after his arrival, a Zemindar of Kadampur, named Debendra Chandra Mitra, sued one of his ryots for ejectment in the local Múnsiff's Court. Nalini espoused the defendant's cause and showed so stout a fight that the case was dismissed with costs. Debendra Babu was deeply offended with the young pleader, and determined to do him a bad turn if possible.

About a week later Nalini got a telegram from Benares announcing his mother's death. He promptly donned the customary Kácha (mourning-cloth) and hurried home, only to find his brother, Jadunáth Babu, already in possession of the sad news; and they went to Benares to comfort their stricken father.

After the customary month of mourning Jadu Babu made preparations for celebrating the *srádh* on a grand scale, by giving presents to distinguished Brahmans, feasting his relatives, and distributing alms to the poor. No money was spared in order to keep his mother's memory green. The family's position would have been most enviable, but for a slight unpleasantness which was created by some of the villagers. Debendra Babu, who had been waiting for an opportunity of revenge, went from house to house urging his neighbours not to participate in the *srádh*, on the score that Nalini had married into a strange clan and was *ipso facto* an outcast. Jadu Babu was stung to the quick on learning these machinations. He consulted Nalini as to the best method of parrying them, and was consoled by his brother's assurance that it would be quite easy to win over his opponents except, perhaps, Debendra Babu himself.

When the time for distributing Samájik (gifts) came round, Jadu Babu sent one to every caste-fellow in the village, but all returned them without a word of explanation. Nalini was not so much distressed as he by the rebuff. He advised an attempt to pacify Debendra Babu; which failing, he would put his scheme into execution. The two brothers, therefore, called on their enemy, and falling at his feet, implored him to say how they had offended him.

"You are much better off than I am," replied Debendra Babu sarcastically; "it would be presumptuous for me to consort with such people. You remember the old fable of the earthen pot and brass vessel?"

"Mahásay," pleaded Jadu Babu, "we are young enough to be your sons. If we have unwittingly caused you offence, we beg to be forgiven."

"You have learnt how to talk sweetly enough," rejoined Debendra Babu. "Nalini fancies himself a *Lát* (lord) or *bádsháh* at the very least. What times we live in! The young have no respect whatever for their seniors!"

"Nalini is hardly more than a boy," said Jadu Babu with folded hands. "I am sure he had not the slightest intention of hurting your feelings."

"What's the use of talking nonsense?" growled Debendra Babu. "Go away!" and he pointed to the door.

The brothers did not stir; but Jadu Babu asked, "So you won't overlook our faults, or even tell us what they are?"

"Well, if you will have it," replied Debendra Babu in measured accents, "Nalini is an outcast; and no respectable Kayastha can take part in your mother's *srádh*."

Jadu Babu fairly lost his temper. He exclaimed: "If there is a flaw in my sister-in-law's pedigree, what is to be said of people who visit women of alien religions, take food from their hands, and tipple strong liquor with them?"

This was a home thrust. Debendra Babu was well-known to be carrying on an intrigue with a Mohammadan woman, named Seráji, but as he was well-to-do, no one had dared to propose his excommunication. He started from his feet in an outburst of fury.

"What! you have the audacity to lecture me—a wretched brat like you? Leave my house at once." So saying he flounced into his inner apartments; while the brothers went away rather crestfallen.

After returning home Nalini disclosed his famous scheme for circumventing the boycott, which Jadu Babu heartily approved. To every Samájik they added an envelope containing a new ten-rupee note and sent them round to their caste-fellows. The sight of money banished prejudices; one and all received the gifts, and some were so shameless as to hint that similar largesse would be acceptable to their uncles or cousins.

Debendra Babu was deeply annoyed by the success of the strategy. He swore a mighty oath not to rest until he had destroyed the Basu family root and branch. After a good deal of thought he matured a plan which was to be executed through a notorious widow belonging to the village. This creature, Hiramani by name, had passed middle life and lived on a little money left by her husband, in a hut close to Debendra's residence. People used to say that God had created her a female by oversight, for she had every bad quality which a man could possess. She was noted for the fact that misfortune invariably fell on a house which she honoured with her intimacy. People were very shy indeed of inviting her.

One bright afternoon Hiramani called at the Basus and started a conversation with the wives of Jadu and Nalini by inquiring about their household affairs, and offering advice which is generally acceptable if seldom acted on. While they sat talking Jadu Babu's eldest boy came to his mother, whimpering:—

"*Chota Káká* (my young uncle) has whipped me because an inkpot of his slipped from my hand, while I was playing with it, and got broken!"

"He served you rightly, naughty boy!" observed his mother administering a sharp slap which sent the child off bellowing loudly.

Hiramani remarked, "You ought not to beat him for so trivial a fault".

"That's a terrible boy," explained the mother. "He is up to all manner of tricks, and if he is not checked, he will grow up a regular *Badmásh*."

"God forbid!" remarked Hiramani; "but has he not been too cruelly used by his uncle? You must have noticed the welts on his naked back. I counted five as broad as my forefinger. How could a grown-up man torture a child like that?"—and she looked meaningly at her hostess.

The mother was evidently impressed by these words. She undertook to speak to Nalini about his treatment of her son. Hiramani was delighted to see that the poison was beginning to work. She went straight from the Basus' house to Debendra Babu and reported her success. He praised her warmly, presented her with a rupee, and offered further instructions.

Hiramani soon became a regular visitor of the Basu ladies. She lost no opportunity of poisoning the mind of Jadu Babu's wife, by retailing Nalini's iniquities. At the outset her insinuations were disregarded; but in time the elder wife fell so completely under Hiramani's influence as to accept her stories as gospel truth. One day, indeed, she ventured to ask her husband to separate from his brother and, on meeting with a peremptory refusal, declared that she would take no food while Nalini remained in the house. Finding that she really meant to carry out this awful threat, Jadu Babu apparently yielded, promising to eject his brother. When the villagers saw Hiramani so thick with the Basu ladies, they prophesied ill-luck for the family, and on learning Jadu Babu's resolve they remarked that the old woman had not belied her reputation. As for Nalini, he knew that something was in the wind, but carefully avoided broaching the subject to his brother, lest he should widen the breach. Like a sacrificial goat, he waited for the stroke to fall on his devoted head. Shortly afterwards, Jadu Babu told his wife to make arrangements for setting up a separate establishment. Her heart leapt for joy. She cooked twice the number of dishes usually prepared for her husband's midday meal, and anxiously waited for him in her kitchen.

Jadu Babu went about his duties as usual, never mentioning the coming separation to Nalini. After bathing at 11 A.M. he took Nalini into the latter's kitchen, and asked his sister-in-law to give them something to eat. The pair sat down to a hastily-prepared repast, Jadu Babu chatting and joking with his brother according to his wont. After dinner he took his betel box and adjourned to the parlour for rumination and a siesta. Nalini and his wife were surprised by Jadu Babu's behaviour. They dared not ask him why he had invited himself to eat with them, but waited anxiously for further developments.

Meanwhile the elder wife was eating her heart with vexation and forming resolutions to give her husband a curtain lecture. But he slept that night in the parlour and on the morrow took both meals with Nalini. When a woman fails to gain her object she is apt to take refuge in tears, which are generally enough to force a mere man to bend to her wishes. Jadu's wife watched for an opportunity of having it out with her husband. On finding him alone, she burst into lamentations, beating her heart and praying that God would put an end to her wretched life. He calmly asked what was the matter and, on receiving no reply, went to bed. Presently she asked, "What has induced you to put me to shame?" Jadu Babu pretended ignorance, and thus made her only the more angry.

"Oh, you *Neka*" (buffoon), she groaned, "didn't you swear to separate from Nalini, and have you not taken all your meals with him ever since? Is that the action of a truthful man?"

"Well, I should like to know how Nalini has injured me?"

"I say that he is your enemy!"

"Tut, tut, you ought to be ashamed of yourself! Where could I find a brother so faithful and obedient as he? You wish to live apart from him? Very well; I have made separate arrangements for you." Then in dispassionate tones Jadu Babu pointed out the treachery of Debendra and his parasite. The woman's eyes were opened. She fell at her husband's feet and implored his pardon. Then she suddenly rose, went across the courtyard to Nalini's room, and knocked at his door. He came out and, seeing his sister-in-law there at an unusual hour, asked anxiously whether Jadu was ill. She reassured him and took him by the hand to his brother, in whose presence she asked him to forgive and forget the offence. Nalini was nothing loth; and harmony was soon restored in the family.

Meanwhile old Hiramani had not failed to report progress to her patron daily. He was delighted to think that the rift in the Basu lute was widening, and promised her a handsome reward when the estrangement should take place.

On learning the failure of the plot, he paid Hiramani a surprise visit, abused her roundly, and, when she retorted in the like strain, he administered a wholesome correction with his shoe. On his departure she ran to Jadu Babu's house intending to have it out with his wife for her breach of faith. The doorkeeper, however, roughly denied her entrance; and when she threatened to report him to his mistress, he ran her out by the neck. Hiramani went home in a state of impatient anger and despair, and for several days she dared not show her face in the village. The spell cast by her malice was broken.

DEBENDRA BABU IN TROUBLE.

One chilly morning in February a Mohammadan neighbour of Nalini's named Sadhu Sheikh burst into his parlour crying, "Chota Babu, Chota Babu (lit. 'little babu,' used for younger brother, to distinguish him from the elder, styled 'bara babu'), Siráji is dying!"

"Who is she?" asked Nalini looking up from a law book which he was studying.

"Surely you know my sister, Chota Babu?"

"Yes, of course, what's the matter with her?"

"She has been ill for three days, with excruciating internal pains; what am I to do, Bábuji?"

"Who is treating her?" asked Nalini.

"Abdullah has been giving her the usual remedies."

"Why, he is a peasant and knows nothing of medicine. You should not have called him in."

"Sir, we are poor folk. Abdullah is very clever and his fee is a mere trifle."

"What drugs has he been administering?"

"*Homopotik* (homoeopathic), they are called."

"Now you had better return home at once to find out how she is progressing. Let me know if she grows worse and I will send Hriday Doctor. Don't trouble about his fees; I will pay them myself. Why did you not come to me earlier?"

Sadhu muttered some words, which Nalini could not distinguish, and left the room hurriedly. After waiting for an hour for news, Nalini threw a wrapper over his shoulders and went to Siráji's cottage. On nearing it he learnt from Sadhu's loud lamentations that she was beyond the reach of medicine; so, after a few words of sympathy, he went home.

Presently Sadhu sallied forth to ask the neighbours' help in carrying the dead body to burial. One and all refused to lay a hand on it because, they said, she had lived with an unbeliever. In dire distress Sadhu again appealed to Nalini, who summoned the chief inhabitants of the Musalmánpára (Mohammadan quarter) to his house and ordered them to take Siraji's body to the burial ground. They reluctantly agreed to do so, and assembled at Sadhu's cottage; but at the last moment all of them refused to touch the corpse. Nalini was puzzled by their behaviour. He asked for an explanation, whereon the Mohammadans whispered together and nudged a grey-beard, who became their spokesman.

"Mahásay," he said, "the fact is Siráji lived with Debendra Babu and was actually made *enceinte* by him. In order to save himself from exposure and shame, Debendra Babu got Abdullah to administer powerful drugs to the woman. After taking these she was attacked by violent pains in the abdomen and vomiting, which ended in her death. The Chaukidar (village watchman) knows all the facts, and he is sure to give information to the police. You know, sir, that no one would dare to touch a corpse without their permission, if there is any suspicion of foul play."

Nalini was greatly surprised; he asked Sádhu whether the old man's words were true and, getting no reply except a significant silence, said: "You may now go about your business, but mind I shall expect you all to assemble here and carry Siráji to the burial ground as soon as the police give you leave to do so".

There was a chorus of assent, and the crowd dispersed. Nalini was about to return home too, when the Chaukidar came in and told him that he had reported Siráji's death to the Sub-Inspector of police, who had ordered him not to permit the corpse to be touched by any one until his arrival.

About three o'clock on the same day Nalini heard that the police had come to investigate the cause of Siráji's death. He went at once to Sádhu's house, where the Sub-Inspector was recording the statements of eye-witnesses. When Abdullah's turn came, the police officer surveyed him from head to foot, saying:—

"I have heard of you before; what is your occupation?"

"Sir, I am a Hakim (doctor)."

"Anything else?"

"Yes, sir, I have a little cultivation and sometimes lend money."

"Did you attend the deceased woman?"

"Yes, I was called in by Sádhu a week ago, and treated her for fever."

"A nice mess you have made of the case too! Swear on the Quran that you gave her no poison or drug!"

"Sir, I am ready to declare in the name of God and His Prophet that I gave her nothing but *homopotik,* only *nuxo bomicka* (nux vomica) in doses which would not have harmed a baby."

"Now, remember you are on your oath. Did you administer anything else?"

Abdullah's shaking limbs proved that he was terribly apprehensive of evil consequences to himself. He muttered, "I gave her a little *patal*-juice too."

"So I thought," said the Sub-Inspector. "Now all present will follow me." With the assistance of his constable and chaukidars, he led them to Debendra Babu's house. The latter received them in his parlour. He affected to be surprised and shocked by the news of Siráji's death.

"That is strange," retorted the Sub-Inspector. "Abdullah here has sworn that he poisoned her at your request."

Debendra Babu became ashen pale, but he soon regained self-possession. Turning on Abdullah he shouted:—"How dare you say that I gave you any such orders?"

"Babu," whined Abdullah, "I never said so. The Darogaji is mistaken."

The Sub-Inspector perceived that, all the witnesses being tenants of Debendra Babu, there was no hope of getting them to stick to any statement inculpating him. He sulkily told the Mohammadans present that they might bury Siráji's corpse, and accompanied Debendra Babu to his house, where he was royally entertained till next morning. However, on taking leave, he hinted that enough evidence had been secured to warrant his reporting the case as one of causing abortion by means of drugs, and that the *Pulis Saheb* (District Superintendent) would probably order further investigation. Debendra Babu was seriously alarmed by the implied threat. Visions of jail—perchance transportation across the dark ocean—floated in his sensorium. He resolved to submit the case to an astrologer.

Gobardhan Chakravarti was an old Brahman neighbour who lived by casting nativities, giving weather and crop forecasts, and prophesying good or evil things in proportion to the fee he received. Debendra Babu paid him a visit next morning and was received with the servile courtesy due to a wealthy client. After beating about the bush for a while he said: "My fate just now seems very unpropitious; when may I expect better times?"

Gobardhan covered a slate with mysterious calculations and, after poring over them for ten or fifteen minutes, he looked up with the remark:—"Your luck is really atrocious and has been so for more than three months."

"Quite true, but what I want to know is—how long is this going to last?"

"I am afraid that you may expect one misfortune after another; I can't quite see the end of your evil destiny."

"Goodness gracious! what shall I do? Are there no means of conjuring it away?"

"Certainly, the Shástras prescribe certain *Grahasanti* (propitiation of planets) processes, which will enable you to counteract the influence of malign stars."

The cunning bait was swallowed by Debendra Babu, who asked: "How much would these ceremonies cost?"

After thinking out the maximum amount he could decently demand, the astrologer said: "About one hundred rupees."

"Oh, that's far too much," was the reply. "Do you want to ruin me? Can't you do it for less?"

"Not a pice less. I could perform a *jog* (sacrifice) for as little as ten rupees; but such maimed rites are quite contrary to the Shástras."

"Will you guarantee definite results for Rs. 100?" asked Debendra Babu anxiously.

"I promise nothing; if you have faith in my ceremonies, you must pay me my own price; if not—I leave you to Fate."

"I have implicit faith in you," groaned Debendra Babu, who was now terribly alarmed, "and will pay you Rs. 100 to-morrow, but please don't delay; the matter is very pressing."

Gobardhan agreed to the proposal; but seeing that his client was loth to go and evidently had something on his mind, he remarked:—

"When a wise man consults a physician, he always discloses his symptoms. You must be quite frank and tell me how your affairs have been progressing lately, in order that I may address my incantations to the proper quarter. Be sure that I will divulge nothing."

Thus encouraged Debendra Babu revealed his relations with Siráji, confessed that he had bribed Abdullah to administer a powerful drug to her, and expatiated on the very awkward predicament in which her sudden death had placed him.

Gobardhan listened with breathless attention and then remarked: "You have acted rightly in telling me the whole truth. I will perform a *homa* (burnt sacrifice) and verily believe that it will have the desired effect. Let me have Rs. 200 and I will set about it at once."

Debendra Babu groaned inwardly at the thought of so heavy an expenditure; but after all, the prospect of escaping deadly peril was well worth Rs. 200. So he returned home and thence despatched the amount in currency notes to Gobardhan.

The astrologer spent about Rs. 5 on *ghi* (clarified butter), rice, and plantains for his *homa* sacrifice, and completed it in three days. Then he called on the police Sub-Inspector, who received him cordially. After the usual compliments had been exchanged, Gobardhan asked how his host was faring.

"Things are not going well with me," was the reply. "Most of the people in those parts are miserably poor; and what I can extract from the well-to-do hardly suffices for my horse-keep. *Thákurji* (a term used in addressing Brahmans), I want you to examine my palm and say when good times are coming for me."

After poring over the proffered hand for fully a minute, muttering and shaking his head the while, Gobardhan said: "I am delighted to tell you that your good star is in the ascendant. Very soon you will make something handsome."

"I wish I could think so!" observed the policeman, "but it is impossible. I have only one likely case on my file, and prospects are not brilliant even in that quarter."

Then, in answer to leading questions from Gobardhan, he told the story of Siráji's death—adding that he had decided to send Debendra Babu and Abdullah up for trial, but doubted whether he could adduce sufficient evidence to convict them of murder or anything like it.

Gobardhan asked: "Now, why should you lose such a splendid opportunity of making money?" and seeing the policeman's eyes twinkle, he went on, "Oh, you need not appear in this transaction yourself. I will do the needful. Tell me frankly—how much money would satisfy you?"

"I could not run the risk of reporting the case as false for less than Rs. 100."

"That is too much," was the wily astrologer's reply. "Mention a reasonable sum, and I will see what can be done."

"Well, I will take Rs. 75, and not a pice less; and understand, if the money is not paid before this evening, I will send Debendra Babu up for trial."

"Very good; I will call on him at once and frighten him into paying up; but I must have something for myself."

"Certainly, if you can get Rs. 75 from the defendant you may keep Rs. 15 as commission."

Gobardhan returned home, took the required amount from the Rs. 200 paid him by Debendra Babu, and handed it privately to the Sub-Inspector, who swore by all the gods that he would take no further steps against the inculpated men.

Knowing well that the policeman would keep faith with a Brahman, Gobardhan went straight to Debendra Babu with the glad news that the *homa* sacrifice had been completely successful, and not a hair of his head would be injured. Debendra felt as though a mountain was lifted from his heart; he stooped to wipe the dust from Gobardhan's feet.

On learning a few days later that the case had been reported to headquarters as false, he was firmly convinced that Gobardhan's magical rites had saved him from ruin, and presented him with a bonus of Rs. 50. Nalini Babu was not long in ascertaining how the land lay. He was exasperated by the sordid wrong-doing which reached his ears and resolved to report it to the District Magistrate. But in the end he kept silent, because Sadhu came to him with tearful eyes, saying that he had already suffered deep humiliation; and if old scandals were raked up, the community would certainly excommunicate him.

TRUE TO HIS SALT.

Hiramani did not forget the thrashing given her by Debendra Babu for failing to cause a rupture between the Basu brothers. She took a vow of vengeance and laid in wait for an opportunity of fulfilling it. Meeting him one day in the village street, she asked with an air of mystery:—

"Have you heard the news?"

"What's that?" replied Debendra Babu carelessly.

"It concerns the woman Siráji," she whispered.

All Debendra Babu's fears revived; he exclaimed: "Speak plainly, what is the matter?"

"The matter stands thus. You know that her case was hushed up by the police? Well, I hear on good authority that the District Magistrate has received an anonymous letter relating the real cause of her death and has ordered a fresh investigation. So I am afraid you will soon be in hot water again. As I am your well-wisher in spite of the cruel treatment I have received, I think it my duty to warn you of this new danger."

Hiramani spoke in faltering accents and wiped away an imaginary tear with the corner of her cloth.

"How did yon learn all this?" asked Debendra Babu in deep anxiety.

"I got the news only last night from the wife of the new Sub-Inspector who has come here on transfer. On paying my respects to her, I was told in confidence that her husband had orders to make a searching inquiry into the cause of Siráji's death."

Debendra Babu saw that his secret was at the woman's discretion. He answered in an apologetic tone: "It was certainly foolish of me to lose my temper with you, but I had some provocation. Forgive me, and let bye-gones be bye-gones. Whom do you suspect of sending the anonymous letter?"

Hiramani bit her lips; she knew the author, who was none other than herself, and replied: "It might have been written by Jadu Babu; but I suspect his brother Nalini, who is as venomous as a snake and hates you mortally".

Debendra Babu stamped his foot in annoyance and, after musing awhile, asked, "What would you advise me to do?"

Hiramani wagged her head sententiously. "Babuji, I am afraid you are in a serious scrape. The matter has gone too far to be hushed up a second time. You cannot do anything directly without increasing the suspicion which attaches to you; but I will watch events and keep you informed of all that happens at the police station. You know I have friends there."

Debendra Babu was profuse in his thanks. He pressed a couple of rupees into the old woman's willing palm, saying: "Hiramani, I see that you are really my well-wisher. Come to my house as often as you like; and if you have anything particular to say to me, I shall always be glad to hear it—and grateful too."

Then the pair separated, and Hiramani took advantage of the Babu's invitation by visiting his daughter Kamini that very evening.

She was made welcome in the inner apartment and sat down for a long chat, in the course of which she asked after Kamini's husband.

"He has gone out for a stroll," her hostess replied, "but I expect him back every minute."

The words were hardly out of her mouth ere a young man came in hurriedly and, not noticing Hiramani who sat in the shade, asked for a drink of water. Hiramani doubted not that he was Debendra Babu's son-in-law, Pulin by name, who had lately come to live with his wife's family. She introduced herself as a friend of his father-in-law's and, being very witty when she chose to exert herself, soon managed to make a favourable impression on the young man. He asked her to come again whenever she pleased, adding that he was generally at home after sunset.

Hiramani had prepared the ground for a further attack. She left the house with a certainty that she had made a good impression.

Thenceforward hardly a day passed without at least one visit to Debendra Babu's. Hiramani wormed all Kamini's little harmless secrets out of her and obtained enough knowledge of the girl's tastes and habits to serve her own designs.

One day, finding herself alone with Pulin, she threw out dark hints against his wife's character. The young man's suspicion was excited. He pressed for more explicit information, but Hiramani shook her head mysteriously without replying. Pulin insisted on being told the truth, whereon Hiramani poured out a whispered story of Kamini's intrigues, mentioning names of male relatives who were known to frequent the house. Pulin was stung to the quick. Regardless of a stranger's presence, he called Kamini into the room, abused her roundly, and declared that he would never live with her again. Then gathering up a few belongings in a bundle, he quitted the house, leaving his wife in a flood of tears. Hiramani was overjoyed by the results of her machinations. She affected sympathy with the deserted wife, who was too young and innocent to suspect her of having caused the quarrel.

Debendra Babu had a servant, Rám Harak by name, who had been in the family for nearly forty years and was treated as one of them. He had watched the growing intimacy between Hiramani and the young couple and, knowing the old woman's character well, endeavoured to counteract her evil influence. Finding this impossible he sought Debendra Babu in the parlour, salámed profoundly, and stood erect, without uttering a word. His master asked, with some surprise, what he wanted.

"Mahásay," replied Rám Harak, "have I not served you for two-score years with obedience and fidelity? Have you ever found me untrue to my salt?"

"Certainly not; I know you are a good and faithful servant."

"Then, Mahásay, you ought to protect me against enemies of your house. That odious hag, Hiramani, has abused me foully."

"Now, Rám Harak, it is you who are abusive. What have you done to offend her?"

"You are my father and mother," replied Rám Harak with his eyes full of tears. "Let me explain fully. I have long since suspected Hiramani of making mischief in this house, and have kept a close watch on her movements. The very day of Pulin Babu's departure I overheard her whispering all manner of false insinuations against my young mistress. Then came the quarrel between husband and wife, which ended in Pulin Babu's leaving your house. After he had gone I ventured to remonstrate with Hiramani for poisoning *jamai* (son-in-law) Babu's mind against his wife; whereon she overwhelmed me with abuse and actually threatened to get me dismissed! I want to know whether this woman is mistress of the family? Am I to have no redress?"

"Leave all this to me, Rám Harak, and go to your work. I'll speak to Hiramani myself."

"Babuji, you are treating the matter far too lightly. I would never have complained on my own account, but I cannot bear to see her plotting against your daughter's happiness, which she has, perhaps, destroyed for ever!"

Debendra Babu went into his inner apartments and, seeing Hiramani engaged in close conversation with his daughter, he asked her why she had used bad language to Rám Harak. The old woman beckoned him to come outside; and after making sure that no one was listening, she poured into his ears a long tale of Rám Harak's misdoings. He was robbing his master, she declared, taking *dasturi* (commission on purchases) at twice the customary rates. What was far worse, the "faithful servant" had spoken freely of Debendra Babu's relations with Siráji in the village, and it was he who instigated the anonymous letter which was about to bring the police down on his master. Though all this was the purest fiction, Debendra Babu swallowed it greedily. He shouted for Rám Harak and, on the man's appearance, charged him with fraud and unfaithfulness to his salt. Rám Harak stood silent with folded hands, not deigning to exculpate himself, which so enraged Debendra Babu that he gave the poor old man a sharp blow on the head with his shoe, bidding him begone and never to cross his threshold again. Rám Harak went to his hut, collected his possessions in a bundle, and left the house where forty years of his life had been spent. Hiramani's plans of vengeance were prospering.

Soon after these unpleasant events the new Sub-Inspector of police arrived at Debendra Babu's house with a warrant for his arrest, and took him to the station despite loud protests of innocence. There he applied for bail, which was of course refused, and he spent the night in the lock-up. Knowing well that he had a very bad case, he humbled himself so far as to send for Nalini, whom he implored with folded hands to save him from destruction. Nalini was deeply moved by his appeal. He heartily despised the fellow's unutterable baseness, but reflected that he had been an old friend of his father's. He undertook the prisoner's defence.

In due course Debendra Babu, with Abdullah, was brought before the Deputy Magistrate of Ghoria on various grave charges. The evidence established a strong *prima facie* case against both, and Nalini Babu reserved his defence. They were committed for trial. When the case came before the Sessions Judge the Government Pleader (public prosecutor) adduced many witnesses proving the prisoner's guilt, the last of whom was Hiramani, who admitted on cross-examination that she had caused the anonymous letter to be sent to headquarters, which led to the charge being reopened. She protested that she had done so from a feeling that so great a crime should not be hushed up. Nalini Babu, in his turn, put forward some witnesses for the defence; but their statements were not of material advantage to the prisoner. It was, in fact, a losing game, but he played it manfully. After all evidence had been recorded, the Government Pleader was about to sum up for the prosecution, when the Court rose suddenly, as it was past five o'clock.

Nalini was going homewards in the dusk, when he felt a hand laid timidly on his shoulder. Turning sharply round, he saw an old man standing by his side. On being asked his name and business, the newcomer whispered some information which must have interested Nalini greatly for he rubbed his hands, smiled, and nodded several times. After a few minutes' talk the pair went together to a spot where a palanquin with bearers was waiting. Into it got Nalini and was carried off at a smart trot, while his companion hobbled behind.

When the Court assembled next day Nalini thus addressed the judge: "May it please your honour, I have, by the greatest good luck, obtained certain evidence which will, I think, place this case in a new light." On getting leave to adduce an additional witness, he beckoned to an old man, standing at the back of the Court, who entered the witness-box and declared that his name was Rám Harak and that he was a dismissed servant of the prisoner. This was a curious opening for a witness for the defence, and dead silence fell on the Court while Rám Harak proceeded to swear that it was he, and not Debendra Babu, who had been intimate with the deceased, and that she had poisoned herself to avoid excommunication.

"Did she tell you so herself?" asked the judge sharply.

"No, your highness; I learnt this only yesterday from Maina Bibi, Karim's own sister; Piyari Bibi, Sádhu's daughter; and Nasiban Bibi, his sister-in-law, who all lived with the deceased."

The Government Pleader at once objected to this statement being recorded, as it was hearsay. Nalini, however, assured the judge that the eye-witnesses were in attendance, and called them, one by one, to give evidence. Passing strange was their story. On the evening of Siráji's death they found her writhing in agony on the floor and, on being questioned, she gasped out that she could bear her kinsfolks' tyranny no longer. They had just told her that she was to be excommunicated for intriguing with an infidel. So she had got some yellow arsenic from the domes (low-caste leather-dressers) and swallowed several *tolas* weight of the poison in milk. The other women were thunderstruck. They sat down beside her and mingled their lamentations until Siráji's sufferings ended for ever. They afterwards agreed to say nothing about the cause of her death for fear of the police. But Rám Harak had come to them privately and frightened them into promising to tell the whole truth, by pointing out the awful consequences of an innocent man's conviction. Their evidence was not shaken by the Government Pleader's cross-examination, and it was corroborated by a dome, who swore that Siráji had got some arsenic from him a few days before her death, on the pretext that it was wanted in order to poison some troublesome village dogs. After consulting with the jury for a few minutes, the judge informed Nalini that his client was acquitted, and Debendra Babu left the Court, as the newspapers say, "without a stain on his character". Seeing Rám Harak standing near the door with folded hands, he clasped the good old man to his bosom, with many protestations of gratitude, and begged him to forgive the injustice with which he had been treated.

When Rám Harak found himself alone with his master at the close of this exciting day, he repeated the vile insinuations which Hiramani had made regarding the daughter's character. Debendra Babu was highly indignant and vowed that the scandal-monger should never cross his threshold again. He then implored Rám Harak to trace his son-in-law, authorising him to offer any reparation he might ask. The old man smiled, and left the house, but returned a quarter of an hour later with a Sanyási (religious mendicant) who revealed himself as the missing Pulin. Debendra Babu received him with warm embraces and many entreaties for pardon; while Pulin said modestly that he alone was to blame, for he ought not to have believed the aspersions cast on his wife by Hiramani, which led him to quit the house in disgust. He added that Rám Harak had found him telling his beads near a temple, and persuaded him to wait close at hand until he had opened Debendra Babu's eyes.

Meanwhile the whole house echoed with songs and laughter. Debendra Babu rewarded Rám Harak's fidelity with a grant of rent-free land, and publicly placed a magnificent turban on his head. He resolved to celebrate his own escape from jail by feasting the neighbours. The entire arrangements were left in the hands of the two Basus, who managed matters so admirably that every one was more than satisfied and Debendra Babu's fame was spread far and wide. When things resumed their normal aspect, he held a confab with the brothers as to the punishment which should be meted out to Hiramani, and it was unanimously resolved to send her to Coventry. They, therefore, forbade the villagers to admit her into their houses, and the shopkeepers to supply her wants. Hiramani soon found Kadampur too hot to hold her and took her departure for ever, to every one's intense relief.

A TAME RABBIT.

When a penniless Hindu marries into a wealthy family he is sorely tempted to live with, and upon, his father-in-law. But the ease thus secured is unattended by dignity. The *gharjamái*, "son-in-law of the house," as he is styled, shocks public opinion, which holds it disgraceful for an able-bodied man to eat the bread of idleness. Pulin incurred a certain degree of opprobrium by quartering himself on Debendra Babu; neighbours treated him with scant courtesy, and the very household servants made him feel that he was a person of small importance. He bore contumely with patience, looking forward to the time when Debendra Babu's decease would give him a recognised position. His wife was far more ambitious. She objected strongly to sharing her husband's loss of social standing and frequently reproached him with submitting to be her father's *annadás* (rice-slave).

So, one morning, he poured his sorrows into Nalini's sympathetic ear.

"Mahásay," he said, "you know that people are inclined to blame me for living in idleness, and I do indeed long to chalk out a career for myself. But I don't know how to set about it and have no patron to back me. Do you happen to know of any job which would give me enough to live on? Salary is less an object with me than prospects. I would gladly accept a mastership in some high school."

"You are quite right in seeking independence," replied Nalini, "and I shall be glad to help you. But lower-grade teachers are miserably paid, and their prospects are no better. It is only graduates who can aspire to a head-mastership. Are you one?"

"No, sir, but I passed the F.A. examination in 1897."

"Ah, then, you are a Diamond Jubilee man—that's a good omen," rejoined Nalini, with a shade of sarcasm in his voice. "What were your English text-books?"

"I read Milton's *Absalom and Achitophel*, Dryden's *Holy Grail*, and many other poems, but I'm not sure of their titles after all these years."

Nalini suspected that his friend's English lore was somewhat rusty. In order to test him further, he asked, "Can you tell me who wrote 'Life is real, life is earnest,'—that line applies to you!"

Pulin fidgeted about before answering. "It must have been Tennyson—or was it Wordsworth? I never could keep poetry in my head."

Nalini thought that an F.A. might have remembered Longfellow's *Psalm of Life*, but he refrained from airing superior knowledge.

"Do you know any mathematics?" he inquired.

"Mathematics!" replied Pulin joyously. "Why, they're my *forte*—-I am quite at home in arithmetic, algebra, and geometry. Please ask me any question you like."

"Well, let us have Prop. 30, Book I. of Euclid."

Pulin rattled off Proposition 13 of that book, without the aid of a diagram. Nalini now saw that the young man's mental equipment was of the slenderest description. He said, "Well, you may call on me another day, when I may be able to tell you of some vacancy".

Pulin, however, would take no denial. He became so insistent that Nalini reluctantly gave him a letter of introduction to Babu Kaliprasanna Som, Secretary of the Rámnagar High School, who, he said, was looking about him for a fourth master. Pulin lost no time in delivering it and was immediately appointed to the vacant post.

English education in Bengal is not regarded as a key which opens the door of a glorious literature, but simply and solely as a stepping-stone in the path of worldly success. The Department seems to aim at turning out clerks and lawyers in reckless profusion. Moreover, academic degrees are tariffed in the marriage market. The "F.A." commands a far higher price than the "entrance-passed," while an M.A. has his pick of the richest and prettiest girls belonging to his class. Hence parents take a keen interest in their boys' progress and constantly urge them to excel in class. With such lessons ringing in his ears, the Bengali schoolboy is consumed with a desire to master his text-books. The great difficulty is to tear him away from them, and insist on his giving sufficient time to manly games. When a new teacher takes the helm, he is closely watched in order to test his competence. The older lads take a cruel pleasure in plying him with questions which they have already solved from the Dictionary. Pulin did not emerge from this ordeal with credit, and the boys concocted a written complaint of his shortcomings, which they despatched to the Secretary of the School Committee. The answer was a promise to redress their grievances.

At 10.30 next morning Kaliprasanna Babu entered Pulin's classroom and stood listening to his method of teaching English literature. Presently one of the boys asked him to explain the difference between "fort" and "fortress". After scratching his head for fully half a minute he replied that the first was a castle defended by men, while the second had a female garrison! The Secretary was quite satisfied. He left the room and sent Pulin a written notice of dismissal. The latter was disheartened beyond measure by this unkind stroke of fortune. He shook the dust of Rámnagar from his feet and returned home to lay his sorrows before Nalini, seasoning the story with remarks highly derogatory to Kaliprasanna Babu's character. In order to get rid of an importunate suitor Nalini gave him another letter of introduction, this time to an old acquaintance named Debnath Lahiri who was head clerk in the office of Messrs. Kerr & Dunlop, one of the largest mercantile firms of Calcutta. Pulin was heartily sick of school-mastering, and the prospect of making a fortune in business filled his soul with joy. He borrowed Rs. 30 from Debendra Babu and took the earliest train for Calcutta. On arriving there he joined a mess of waifs and strays like himself, who herded in a small room and clubbed their pice to provide meals. Then he waited on Debnath Babu, whom he found installed in a sumptuous office overlooking the river Hughli. The great man glanced at his credentials and, with an appearance of cordiality, promised to let him know in case a vacancy occurred in the office. For nearly a month Pulin called daily for news at Messrs. Kerr & Dunlop's, and generally managed to waylay the head clerk, whose reply was invariably, "I have nothing to suit you at present".

One morning, however, he was stopped by the darwán (doorkeeper) who told him gruffly that the "Bara Babu did not like to have outsiders hanging about the office". The baffled suitor reflected on his miserable position. He had just eleven rupees and two pice left, which he calculated would last him, with strict economy, for another fortnight. When they were spent, he would have to return crestfallen to Kadampur. But could he face the neighbours' sneers, the servants' contumely—worse than all, his wife's bitter tongue? No, that was not to be thought of. It were better to plunge into the river whose turbid waters rolled only a few feet away.

Pulin was roused from this unpleasant train of thought by hearing his name pronounced. It came from a well-dressed man, who was just entering Messrs. Kerr & Dunlop's office, welcomed by a salám from the surly doorkeeper. Pulin was delighted to recognise in the stranger a certain Kisari Mohan Chatterji, who had taught him English in the General Assembly's College more than a decade back. In a few words he told his sad story and learnt that Kisari Babu had taken the same step as he himself contemplated, with the result that he was now head clerk in Messrs. Kerr & Dunlop's export department. This news augured well for his own ambition, but poor Pulin was disgusted on hearing that no less than three vacancies had occurred in as many weeks, and that all had been filled by relatives of Babu Debnath Lahiri. Kisari Babu added: "A junior clerk is to be appointed to-morrow. Write out an application in your very best hand, with copies of your testimonials, and bring it to me here this evening at five. I'll see that it reaches our manager, Henderson Saheb." Pulin punctually followed his friend's advice, and dreamed all night of wealth beyond a miser's utmost ambition.

On arriving at Messrs. Kerr & Dunlop's office next morning he joined a crowd of twenty or thirty young men who were bent on a like errand. His spirits sank to zero, nor were they raised when after hanging about in the rain for nearly two hours the aspirants were told that the vacancy had been filled up. Thereupon the forlorn group dispersed, cursing their ill-luck and muttering insinuations against Mr. Henderson and his head clerk. Pulin, however, lingered behind. By tendering a rupee to the doorkeeper he got a slip of paper and pencil, with which he indited a piteous appeal to Kisari Babu, and a promise that it should reach him. Presently his friend came out in a desperate hurry, with a stylograph behind his ear, and his hands laden with papers.

"It's just as I anticipated," he whispered to Pulin. "The head clerk has persuaded Henderson Saheb to bestow the post on his wife's nephew. But don't be disheartened. I will speak to our Saheb about you this very day. Come here at five to learn the result."

Pulin did so and was overjoyed to find that he had been appointed probationary clerk in the export department on Rs. 20 per mensem, in supersession of Debnath Babu's nominee.

On the morrow he entered on his new duties with some trepidation, but Kisari Babu took him under his wing and spared no pains to "teach him the ropes". Pulin spent his evenings in furbishing up his English and arithmetic, mastered the whole art of book-keeping, and, being naturally intelligent, he soon had the office routine at his fingers' ends. He grasped the fact that a young man who wishes to succeed in life must make himself indispensable. In course of time Pulin's industry and trustworthiness attracted the attention of Mr. Henderson, who confirmed him as clerk, with a salary of Rs. 35.

But every cup has its bitter drop; and Pulin's was the persistent enmity of the head clerk, who bore him a grudge for ousting his wife's nephew and seized every opportunity of annoying him. Leagued with the arch-enemy were two subordinate clerks, Gyánendra and Lakshminarain by name, who belonged to Debnath Babu's *gústi* (family). This trio so managed matters that all the hardest and most thankless work fell to Pulin's lot. He bore their pin-pricks with equanimity, secure in the constant support of Kisari Babu.

One muggy morning in August he awoke with a splitting headache, the harbinger of an attack of fever, and was obliged to inform the head clerk, by means of a note, of his inability to attend office. An answer was brought by Gyánendra to the effect that three days' leave of absence was granted, but that his work must be carried on by some other clerk. He was, therefore, ordered to send the key of his desk by the bearer. For three days the patient endured alternations of heat and cold; but his malady yielded to quinine, and on the fourth he was able to resume work.

Soon after reaching the office, he was accosted by one of the bearers, named Rámtonu, who told him that *the Bara Saheb*wished to see him at once. The moment he entered the manager's sanctum he saw that something unpleasant had occurred. Without wishing him good morning, as usual, Mr. Henderson handed him a cheque and asked sternly whether he had filled it up. Pulin examined the document, which turned out to be an order on the Standard Bank to pay Tárak Ghose & Co. Rs. 200, signed by Mr. Henderson. He was obliged to admit that the payee's name, as also the amount in words and figures, seemed to be in his handwriting.

"Yes," rejoined the manager, "and the signature is very like my own; but it is a forgery. Do you hear me, Babu, a FORGERY!"

To Pulin's disordered senses the room, with its furniture and Mr. Henderson's angry face, seemed to be turning round. He gasped out, "I'm ill, sir!" and sank into a chair. The manager mistook the remains of fever for a tacit admission of guilt. He waited till Pulin had regained a share of his wits and said gravely: "I did not think that one whom I trusted with my cheque-book would act thus. Now you will search your books, to see whether they contain a record of any payment of the kind, and return with them in half an hour. But I must warn you that if this forgery is traced to you, I shall have to call in the police."

Pulin staggered back to his room in despair and observed that Gyánendra and Lakshminarain, who sat at the next desk, were evidently enjoying his mental agony. Alas! the books showed no trace of any payment to Tárak Ghose & Co. He wrung his hands in great distress and sat bewildered, until Rámtonu came to summon him to the manager's tribunal. In the corridor Rámtonu glanced round, to make sure that no one was within hearing, and said, "Don't be afraid, Babuji. You did me a good turn, and I may be able to help you now."

This Rámtonu was an office menial hailing from the district of Gáyá, in Behar. He was an intelligent man, but rather unlicked, and was the butt of the younger clerks, who delighted in mocking his uncouth up-country dialect. Pulin, however, had never joined in "ragging" him, and, on one occasion, he lent Rámtonu Rs. 7 for his wife, who was about to increase the population of Gáyá. Gratitude for kindness is a marked trait in the Indian character, and Pulin bethought him of the old fable of the Lion and Mouse. He asked: "Why, what do you know about *lekha-para* (reading and writing)?"

"Never mind," rejoined Rámtonu. "We must not loiter, for we should be suspected of plotting together. Come to the Saheb's room. I shall be admitted, for he knows that I don't understand English. All I ask is that you will clasp your hands as a signal when I may come forward and tell my story."

A European police officer was seated by Mr. Henderson's side, engaged in writing from his dictation. They looked up, and the manager asked whether Pulin had found any record of the payment in dispute.

On receiving a negative answer, he said: "Then I shall be obliged to hand you over to the police".

Pulin clasped his hands in a mute appeal for mercy, whereon Rámtonu stepped forward. Carefully extracting a folded sheet of foolscap from the pocket of his *chapkan* (a tight-fitting garment, worn by nearly all classes in full dress), he spread it out on the table and respectfully asked the manager to run his eye over it.

"By Jove," remarked the latter, with great surprise, "here's some one has been copying my signature—and Pulin's writing too!"

All eyes were now bent on the incriminating document. It was made up of many fragments of paper, carefully pasted on a sheet of foolscap, and bore the words, "Tárak Ghose & Co., two hundred rupees, 200," repeated at least twenty times. Below was "A.G. Henderson," also multiplied many-fold. The manager asked where Rámtonu had found the paper, and received the following answer:—"Your Highness, Pulin Babu here did not come to office on Monday; and for the next few days his work was done by Gyánendra Babu, who got the keys of his desk. I knew that he and some other clerks detested Pulin Babu, so I watched their movements narrowly, to see whether they would try to get him into a scrape, and more than once I surprised Gyánendra and Lakshminarain whispering together. On Tuesday neither of them left the office for lunch with the other clerks, and I seized some pretext for entering the room where they sit. Gyánendra roughly bade me begone; so I went to the verandah outside and peeped through the *jilmils* (Venetian blinds) of a window close to their desk. Lakshminarain was copying some English words from a paper on his left side, while the other clerk looked on, nodding and shaking his head from time to time. After writing in this fashion for a while, Lakshminarain took a sheet of notepaper covered with writing and copied the signature many times, until both babus were satisfied with the result. Then I saw Gyánendra unlock Pulin Babu's desk, take out a cheque-book, and hand it to the other man, who filled up the counterfoil and body of one blank cheque, glancing sometimes at the paper in front of him. He returned it to Gyánendra who placed it in a pocket-book. After tearing up the papers they had used and throwing them into the waste-paper basket, they left the room. I ran round, carefully avoiding them, picked the fragments of paper out of the basket, tied them in a corner of my *gamcha* (wrapper), and left the office quickly, asking the doorkeeper what direction they had taken. When he said that they had turned northwards, I guessed that they were off to the Bank, in order to cash the cheque, and sure enough I overtook them not more than a *rassi* from the office. Following them at a little distance on the other side of the street, I saw them stop outside the Standard Bank and look anxiously around. Presently a schoolboy passed by, whom they hailed and, after talking for a while, Gyánendra handed him the cheque with a small linen money-bag, and pointed to the door of the Bank. The lad went inside, while both babus waited round the corner. In a short time he came out and handed the bag full of money to Gyánendra, who gave him something and hurried back to the office with his companion. Putting two and two together I felt assured that those clerks had forged the cheque; and had I known where Pulin Babu lived, I would certainly have communicated my suspicions to him. Having to work without his help, I persuaded a student, who lodges near my quarters, to piece the scraps of paper together. It took him two hours to do so, and we then pasted them carefully on this sheet of foolscap. You will see, Saheb, that there are thirty-seven in all, and only three missing."

The story made a deep impression on Mr. Henderson and the Police Inspector, while Pulin was raised to the seventh heaven of delight by the thought that his innocence might yet be established.

"Could you identify the boy?" asked the Europeans with one breath.

"I don't know his name," was Rámtonu's rejoinder; "but I think I could pick him out, for he passes this office daily on his way to and from school. But this is just the time when he goes home for tiffin. With your Highness's permission, I will watch for him in the street."

"Do so by all means," was the Inspector's reply. "Meanwhile, I'll take down notes of your statement."

Rámtonu went out and in a few minutes returned dragging with him triumphantly a well-dressed lad of fifteen, who seemed terribly alarmed by the company into which he was thrust. The Inspector calmed his fears by assuring him that he would come to no harm if only he spoke the whole truth. "You have been unwittingly made the instrument of a forgery," he added, "and we want your help towards detecting it." The boy plucked up courage and answered every question put him quite candidly. His tale corroborated Rámtonu's in most particulars, with the addition that the tall babu had given him eight annas *bakshish* for cashing the cheque. He had not seen either of the men previously, but thought he should be able to recognise one of them owing to his unusual height.

"Now, bearer," said Mr. Henderson, "go and fetch both the clerks; bring in the tall one first, but keep an eye on the other outside and beyond earshot."

Rámtonu left the room with alacrity and presently returned ushering Lakshminarain into the dreaded presence. The newcomer was beside himself with terror; and when he was identified by the schoolboy as one of the men who had employed him to cash the cheque, he did not wait to be asked for an explanation. Throwing himself at Mr. Henderson's feet he begged for mercy, promising to reveal the entire truth. The Inspector would make no promises but simply adjured him to make a clean breast of his share in the transaction. Lakshminarain obeyed, and his statement, interrupted by many sobs, was duly recorded. His accomplice was next introduced. At first Gyánendra was inclined to put a bold face on the matter, stoutly affirming that it was a put-up affair between Pulin and Rámtonu. When, however, the Inspector read out to him the deposition of the bearer and schoolboy, he saw that the game was up and confessed his misdoings, accusing the head clerk of having prompted them. The culprits were taken in a *ticcá gári* (four-wheeled cab) to the police station Pulin occupying the box, while Rámtonu ran behind.

Well, to cut a long story short, the prisoners stuck to their confession and refunded their ill-gotten gains. They were duly committed to the High Court on charges of forgery and conspiring to accuse an innocent man of the like offence. They both pleaded guilty, and the judge remarked that it was one of the worst cases of the kind he had ever tried. In passing sentence of two years rigorous imprisonment on each prisoner, he added that they would have fared worse but for the patent fact that they had been made catspaws of by some one who kept in the background. As there was no evidence against Debnath Babu, except that of accomplices, he was not prosecuted; but immediately after the trial, Messrs. Kerr & Dunlop dismissed him without notice. Kisari Babu was promoted to the vacant office of head clerk, while Pulin stepped into his friend's shoes. By unfailing application to duty, he won Messrs. Kerr & Dunlop's entire confidence, and in fulness of time succeeded Kisari Babu as head clerk. Ten or twelve years later, Pulin was rich enough to build a *pakka* (masonry) house at Kadampur, which far eclipsed his father-in-law's, and had a well-paid doorkeeper in the person of Rámtonu. The once-despised *gharjamái* took a leading position among the local gentry.

GOBARDHAN'S TRIUMPH.

Jadu Babu's four-year-old daughter, Mrinalini, or Mrinu as she was called in the family, came to her mother one evening to say that her kitten was lost. In vain was she taken on the maternal lap, her tears gently wiped away, and all manner of pretty toys promised. Her little frame was convulsed with sobs, and she refused to be comforted. So her mother sent a maidservant to search for the plaything. The girl returned shortly and said that the kitten was certainly not in the house. At this Mrinu howled more loudly than ever, bringing her father on the scene. He pacified the child by undertaking to produce her pet, and told the servants that the finder would be handsomely rewarded. Meanwhile his wife was trying to keep Mrinu's attention engaged by telling her a long story, when she suddenly exclaimed, "What has become of your *jasam* (gold bracelet)?"

Mrinu replied, "I took it off to play with kitty and laid it down somewhere".

This was all the information she could vouchsafe in answer to repeated questions. The mother set her down and proceeded to search every hole and corner for the *jasam*, but it was not to be found. Her husband was greatly alarmed on hearing of this untoward event. The loss of Rs. 100, at which the trinket was valued, might have been borne; but Hindus believe that misfortune invariably follows the loss of gold. He set all his servants and hangers-on to look for the *jasam*, but they were unsuccessful. In despair he hurried to Nalini for advice and was told to send for Gobardhan, which he promptly did.

The astrologer listened attentively to his story and then asked whether Jadu Babu would try *Báti Chálá* (divination by the *báta* leaf), or some simpler method of discovering the lost *jasam*. On learning that the matter would be left entirely in his hands, he told Jadu Babu to collect all his servants in the parlour and let him have half a seer (1 lb.) of raw rice, with as many strips of banana leaf as there were servants. When all were assembled, Gobardhan thus addressed them, "Mrinu has lost her *jasam*, have any of you seen it?" The reply was a chorus of "Noes" with emphatic head-shakings. "Then none of you have stolen it?" Again a volume of protestations. "Very well, then," said Gobardhan, "I must try the ordeal of chewed rice." After uttering many *mantras* (incantations) and waving his hand over the pile of grain and banana leaves, he dealt out a quotum of each to the servants.

"Now," he said, "you will masticate the rice for a minute thoroughly and then drop the result on your leaves. I warn you that it will be deadly poison for the thief." All obeyed with alacrity, and Gobardhan, after examining the contents of each leaf, assured Jadu Babu that the *jasam* had not been stolen.

My readers who are versed in science will understand that, in point of fact, there is nothing magical about this rite, which is based on the circumstance that fear checks the flow of saliva. In all probability a thief would eject the rice absolutely dry.

The inference was that *the jasam* had been mislaid; and Jadu Babu asked whether Gobardhan's lore was equal to recovering it.

"Possibly," answered the astrologer, "but it is not a case of Báti Chálá; if you can guarantee me Rs. 10, I will perform *Nákha Darpan* (literally 'nail-mirror'). Let me have an almanac, please, to find an auspicious day."

After examining it and receiving a ten-rupee note from Jadu Babu, the astrologer said oracularly that he would return on the following afternoon, with a lad of twelve, who had been born under the Constellation of the Scales.

At the appointed hour, Gobardhan came accompanied by his acolyte, with whom he sat down at the Chandimandab (a shrine of the goddess Durga, found in most Hindu houses, which serves for social gatherings). Jadu Babu and the *bhadralok* (gentle-folk) took their seats there too, while the underlings formed a respectful half-circle in front. Adjuring all to keep perfect silence, he asked the lad to gaze into the nail on his own right index finger and tell the people what he saw there. After staring at it for a minute or so, the boy began to tremble violently and whispered: "I see a mango-tope (orchard); a little girl is playing with her kitten under the trees. Now I see her slipping a *jasam* from her arm, the kitten frisks about, and the child follows it; now it disappears, and the child runs indoors." Then, raising his voice to a shrill scream, he pointed with his left hand to the north and asked:—

"What are those animals which are prowling in the orchard? Are they dogs? No—they are jackals—one, two, three jackals! They pounce on the kitten, and tear her limb from limb! Now everything is growing hazy; I can't see any more!"

A thrill of fear ran through the audience, and one might have heard a pin drop. At length Gobardhan broke the silence:—

"Let us go to the mango-tope north of this house," he said solemnly.

Thither they hurried and, after a few minutes' search, one of the maidservants cried out that she had found the *jasam* half-hidden by the gnarled roots of a tree.

Jadu Babu was overjoyed by the recovery of his missing jewel, and pressed another fee of ten rupees on the astrologer. As for Gobardhan, his fame spread far and wide, and his hut was rarely without some client, eager to learn the future.

PATIENCE IS A VIRTUE.

Sádhu Sheikh of Simulgachi was not long in finding a husband for his half-sister, Maini Bibi. Before she was fourteen, a young farmer named Ramzán proposed for her hand, offering a *den mohur* of Rs. 100. The *den mohur* is a device recognised by Mohammadan law for protecting married women from capricious repudiation. The husband binds himself to refund a fictitious dowry, generally far above his means, in case he should divorce his wife for no fault of hers. Ramzán was accepted by Sádhu, and the marriage was duly celebrated. Maini Bibi was a handsome girl; but beauty was among the least of her gifts. She was sweet-tempered, thrifty, and obedient, winning sympathy on all sides. The one discordant note was struck by Ramzán's mother, Fatima Bibi by name, who took a violent dislike to the bride and evinced it by persistently scolding and ill-using her. Ramzán was completely under his mother's thumb and saw everything with her eyes. His love for Maini was slowly sapped by her innuendoes, and he treated the poor girl with something worse than coldness. Maini, however, bore her hard lot without a murmur, hoping that time and patience would win back her husband's heart.

On returning one evening from the fields, Ramzán was hailed by his mother who was evidently in a worse temper than usual.

"Hi! Ramzán," she shrieked, "I am an old woman, and you, doubtless, find me an incumbrance. Speak out, my son; you have only to say 'go,' and I will leave this house in half an hour."

"Why, what's the matter, mother?" asked Ramzán with open eyes.

"Matter," she yelled. "Would you believe it, that black-faced daughter of a pig has actually abused me—me, your old mother!"

"What did she say?" rejoined Ramzán angrily.

"My son," was the answer, "you know how she neglects household duties, leaving all the hard jobs to me. Well, this afternoon, I ventured on a word of remonstrance, and she actually abused me." And the old woman wiped her tears away with a corner of her cotton wrapper, adding with eyes cast heavenwards, "Merciful Allah, to think that I should come to this in my old age!"

"But what did she say?" repeated Ramzán wearily.

"She told me to my face that I had forgotten to put salt into the curry!"

"That's hardly abusive," rejoined Ramzán.

"You think so," shouted Fatima. "Now you're taking sides with her against your mother, who bore you. You will assuredly suffer in Jehannam (hell) for such a crime! But I'll have it out with that she-devil!"

So saying, she dashed from the room to the kitchen, where the luckless Maini was cowering in anticipation of a coming storm. She was not deceived. Fatima seized her by the hair and administered a sound thumping.

Several days passed by, bringing no alleviation to her fate. But matters came to a crisis on a certain morning, owing to Ramzán's complaint that his wife had over-salted the curry. On tasting the food, Fatima burst into violent imprecations and "went for" her daughter-in-law, who took refuge in the neighbouring brushwood. At nightfall she crept back to the house and found Ramzán closeted with his mother. They were talking earnestly, but Maini could not distinguish the purport of the conversation. It seemed to her that Fatima's voice was raised in entreaty, and Ramzán was objecting to some scheme proposed by her. She passed the night sleepless and in tears.

Early next day Ramzán entered her room and said gruffly, "Get up, collect your chattels, and follow me. I am going to take you back to Sádhu's." Maini obeyed without a word of remonstrance, and a quarter of an hour later the ill-assorted pair might have been seen walking towards Simulgachi.

The rainy season was now in full swing, and their path lay across a deep nullah (ravine) through which mighty volumes of drainage water were finding their way to the Ganges. On reaching a bamboo foot-bridge which spanned it, Ramzán ordered his wife to go first. Ere she reached the opposite bank, he gave her a violent shove, which sent her shrieking vainly for help into the swirling torrent below.

Hardly had Ramzán perpetrated this odious deed than he felt he would give his chances of *bihisht* (paradise) to recall it. He ran along the bank shouting frantically, "Maini! Maini!" Alas! her slender body was carried like a straw by the foaming water towards the Ganges and soon disappeared in a bend of the nullah. Then her murderer sat down and gave himself up to despair. But the sun was up; people were stirring in the fields; and so he slunk homewards. Fatima stood on the threshold and raised her eyebrows inquiringly; but Ramzán thrust her aside, muttering, "It is done," and shut himself up in his wife's room. There everything reminded him of her; the scrupulous neatness of floor and walls—no cobwebs hanging from the rafters, the kitchen utensils shining like mirrors. He sat down and burst into a flood of tears.

For several days he did not exchange a word with his accomplice, and dared not go to market lest his worst fears should be realised. Dread of personal consequences added new torture to unavailing remorse. Every moment he expected the red-pagried ministers of justice to appear and hale him to the scaffold. The position was clearly past bearing. So, too, thought Fatima, for she waylaid her son one afternoon and said: "Ramzán, I cannot stand this life any longer; let me go to my brother Mahmud Sardar, the cooly-catcher".

"Go," he replied sullenly, and the old woman gathered up her belongings in a bundle and departed, leaving him to face the dark future alone.

While brooding over his fate, he was startled by the sudden arrival of Sádhu.

"Now I'm in for it," he thought and began to tremble violently while his features assumed an ashen hue. But Sadhu sat down by his side and said, "Ramzán, I've come about Maini".

"Then she's drowned!" gasped Ramzán. "By Allah the Highest, I swear that I did my best to save her."

"Hullo!" rejoined Sádhu with great surprise; "you must have been with her when she fell into the nullah."

Ramzán bent his head in silence. After a few moments he looked up, clasped his hands, and said:—

"Tell me the truth, Sádhu, is Maini alive?"

"She is," was the reply. "On Thursday morning she came to our house dripping wet and quite exhausted, with a story that your mother had turned her out of doors and that she was on her way to live with us when, on crossing the Padmajali Nullah, her foot slipped and she fell into the water. She told us how, after being carried for nearly a gau-coss (lit. cow league, the distance at which a cow's lowing can be heard), she was swept by the stream against the overhanging roots of a pipal tree *(ficus religiosa)* and managed to clamber up the bank. But Maini never told us that you were with her. Why, Ramzán, you're quaking in every limb. I always suspected Maini had concealed the truth. Swear on the Quran that you did not try to drown her."

Ramzán feebly protested innocence, and the two men sat awhile without speaking.

At length Sádhu said: "I've come to make you a proposal. Young Esáf, the son of Ibrahim of our village, has fallen in love with Maini and wants to marry her. He is willing to pay the *den mohur* of Rs. 100 which would be due from you in case of repudiation. Now we want you to divorce her."

Ramzán was overcome by his wife's magnanimity, and the thought of losing her drove him to distraction. "No!" he shouted, "I won't divorce her. I'll fetch her back this very day!"

"That's quite out of the question," rejoined Sádhu. "Maini cannot bear her mother-in-law's cruelty, and I'm sure she'll never consent to live with you again. Besides, Esáf is a rich man and will make her happy. She shall marry him."

"I say she shan't," said Ramzán emphatically.

Sádhu got up and moved off, remarking, "Very well, I will go to the police station at once and charge you with attempting to kill her! We shall soon worm the truth out of Maini, and get plenty of eye-witnesses too."

Ramzán was beside himself with terror. He followed Sádhu, clasped his feet, and groaned, "No, you won't do that! I am ready to divorce Maini. Let Allah's will be done."

"Ah," replied Sádhu, "so you can listen to reason after all. Come to our house to-morrow evening; we will have witnesses ready, and Esáf will be there with the *den mohur*."

Ramzán had a sleepless night and was too downcast to work on the morrow. When evening came, he walked wearily to Simulgachi. There was quite a small crowd in Sádhu's courtyard. On one side sat Maini and some other women with faces closely covered; Esáf and the witnesses were on the other. Between them was a mat, on which lay a bag full of money. Ramzán was received without salutations, and squatted down by Sádhu's side.

Moslem husbands can get rid of their wives by repeating the word *talaq* (surrender) thrice, in the presence of witnesses. Every one expected him to utter the formula, which would release Maini from his power. However, he sat silent, with downcast eyes. After a minute or two, he rose and, looking steadily at Maini, was just about to speak, when she sprang forward, laid her hand on his arm, and said: "Surely you are not going to divorce me, your faithful wife, who loves you dearly and seeks only to make you happy? What have I done to be treated thus?"

A murmur was heard in the assembly, but Sádhu raised his hand in token of silence.

"Foolish girl!" he exclaimed, "do you wish to return to a mother-in-law who hates and persecutes you? Will Ramzán be able to protect you?" Then lowering his voice, he added, "Is your life safe with those people?"

"Life and death," rejoined Maini, "are in Allah's hands. It is his will that we should fulfil our destinies, and mine is to cling to my husband. I would not change him for Hátim Tái (a legendary hero, very rich and generous) himself!" Then nestling closer to Ramzán, she pleaded in a voice of music, "Surely you don't want to get rid of me?"

He was quite overcome and burst into tears.

"No," he sobbed, "I will never separate from my treasure. Come back to me, and you need not fear my mother's tongue. She has left my house for good, and I swear by Allah, in the presence of all these people, that she shall not live with us again. You, Maini, shall be sole mistress of my house."

Maini was overjoyed by this decision. She clapped her hands twice, and then, picking up the bag of money, said to the crestfallen Esáf, "Take back your rupees; I am going home with my husband".

So speaking, she took Ramzán's hand and led him out of the house, while a great silence fell on the crowd, broken at length by many exclamations and a buzz of loud talk. My readers who know Maini's sweet nature will not be surprised to learn that her happiness was thenceforward without a single cloud.

9 789358 007787

Printed by Libri Plureos GmbH in Hamburg,
Germany